The Dimensions of the Church

Woodstock Papers

Occasional Essays for Theology

PREPARED BY

Professors of the Faculty of Theology
Woodstock College, Woodstock, Maryland

EDITED BY

JOHN COURTNEY MURRAY, S.J.
WALTER J. BURGHARDT, S.J.

No. 8

NEWMAN PRESS

New York   Paramus

THE DIMENSIONS OF THE CHURCH

A Postconciliar Reflection

by AVERY DULLES, S.J.
*Professor of Systematic Theology
Woodstock College*

NEWMAN PRESS

New York   Paramus

Imprimi Potest: EDWARD J. SPONGA, S.J.
Praep. Prov. Marylandiae

Nihil Obstat: VERY REV. MSGR. CARROLL E. SATTERFIELD
Censor Librorum

Imprimatur: LAWRENCE J. SHEHAN, D.D.
Archbishop of Baltimore

January 12, 1967

★ Contents ★

★ Introduction ★

Now that a year has elapsed since its conclusion, one can safely say that Vatican Council II marks one of the great turning points in the history of the Catholic Church. Inevitably the Council has left a turbulent wake behind it. It has provoked eager and sometimes anxious questioning about many crucial matters, and about none so much as the primary theme of its deliberations, the nature and mission of the Church. While many queries are made about particular ecclesiastical structures and activities, Catholics feel most urgently the need for new ways of envisaging the Church as a whole. It will not suffice to substitute one abstract, essential definition for another; what is required is a concrete image which represents the Church within the general framework of human experience and history. The Council itself went a long way toward answering the demand which it created. Its principal documents provide an excellent basis for reflection and discussion about the Church as a society of men fully involved in a diversified and changing world.

During the past year I have had occasion to speak to many audiences—Catholic and Protestant, clerical and lay—about the achievements of the Council. This book grows in part out of such lectures and out of the comments and questions raised by members of the audiences. The various chapters of this work, however, do not precisely reproduce the texts of particular lectures.

The unifying theme of the present work is the Church's relationship to the total human family. The nucleus consists of chapters 2, 3, and 4, which deal with three key areas of confrontation. Chapter 2 considers the Church in relation to the other Christian communities, and thus touches on the theology of ecumenism. Chapter 3 deals with the Church's relationship to the unevangelized peoples, and hence concentrates on missiology. Chapter 4 takes up the goals and activities of the Church in comparison with those of secular institutions; it deals, therefore, with the theology of Christian secularity. These three chapters have an obvious bearing on the three great dialogues in which the Church has recently become engaged, the dialogue (1) with the other Churches, (2) with the other religions, and (3) with what, for lack of a better term, we may call the "world."

Both the urgency and the difficulty of this triple dialogue derive from the paradoxical tension between exclusiveness and inclusiveness which is built into the Christian concept of the Church. For this reason I have thought it appropriate to place at the beginning a chapter entitled "The Dimensions of the Church." Since this chapter is of fundamental importance, I have used its title as that of the book as a whole.

The last chapter explores more deeply, in the light of Dietrich Bonhoeffer's provocative program for a nonreligious Christianity, certain themes already touched on in earlier chapters, especially in chapter 4. Just as all theology between the two world wars had to situate itself in relation to Barth, and, in the decade following World War II, in relation to Bultmann, so, it would seem, Bonhoeffer has now become the indispensable point of reference. This is not simply a question of fashion. The fact is that Bonhoeffer spoke with prophetic urgency—and tantalizing laconicism—about the issues which most insistently force themselves to our attention.

Throughout these pages I have kept in constant view the official statements of Vatican II, and have quoted them frequently. With few exceptions, I have followed the translations of Msgr. Joseph Gallagher in *The Documents of Vatican II* (edited by Walter M. Abbott, S.J.; New York: Guild Press, America Press, and Association Press, 1966).

AVERY DULLES, S.J.

Woodstock College
December 8, 1966

★ 1 ★

The Dimensions of the Church

It is distressing that the community which preaches the most intense charity toward all men often appears to divide its own members from the rest of mankind. It is an unhappy paradox that the religion which most insistently proclaims universal peace and reconciliation often finds itself in a situation of isolation and hostility. In the eyes of the world the Church which prides itself on the name of Catholic (meaning "universal") frequently takes on the appearance of a particular sect. And we must confess, I believe, that most Catholics fail to live up to their name because their own idea of the Church is too small, too narrow, too exclusive. The Second Vatican Council, sensing the growing isolation of Catholics in the modern world, sought to tear down the barriers of distrust and suspicion and to identify the Church with the great concerns of mankind. To achieve this goal, there was no need to forge a new idea of the Church; it was enough to recover the true idea of the Church as established by its divine Founder. In the light of the Vatican documents, and especially the Constitution on the Church, let us ask ourselves what the true dimensions of the Church are. We shall find it a much larger and more inclusive reality than most of us have been accustomed to imagine.

The unique power of the Christian faith to bring men

together into unity was strikingly described by the French Jewish philosopher Henri Bergson in his work *The Two Sources of Morality and Religion* (1932). The central theme of this book is the contrast between two types of society, the closed and the open. The closed society he describes as a particular group turned in upon itself, anxiously concerned for its own survival, one whose members are compelled by force and fear to act for the cohesion of the whole. In such a society the outsider is ignored, misunderstood, scorned, or dreaded; he is regarded as a potential or actual foe. Even religion in the closed society becomes an agent of social cohesion and self-preservation. In Bergson's estimation, the religion of Israel before Christ was largely that of a particular national society, opposed to the Gentiles of the surrounding world. It was a religion of conformity, of the dead letter (although Bergson himself would recognize important qualifications, especially for the prophets). And it is precisely from such a lifeless religion, according to Bergson, that Christ sought to deliver the Jews. By doing away with static, formalistic religion he laid the groundwork for an open society.

The "open society," in Bergson's terminology, is one which excludes no one and nothing; in principle, it welcomes all. It is universal in its tendency and in that sense catholic. But this love of the whole, this unlimited openness, cannot be achieved, Bergson maintains, by progressively expanding the horizons of the group with which a man identifies himself, as though the whole were simply a great organism and an extension of one's own ego. The universal love of humanity, Bergson insists, must necessarily pass through God. It is qualitatively different from all forms of tribal collectivism. Since it demands an authentic gift of self, it presupposes a love which is divine. The religion of the open society, founded on this universal divine love, is dynamic rather than static; its morality rests on the spirit rather than on the letter of the law; yet even this aspiration of charity gives rise to a type of law insofar as love has a logic of its own.

Wherever Christianity is effectively present, and nowhere else, according to Bergson, you have a mysterious gift of self, a restless energy in devotion to the other, unlimited openness, expansiveness, and profound respect for the dignity of the human person. On Bergsonian principles we might conclude at this point that the Church is by nature an open society. It aims not to dominate and subdue others but to accord a maximum of freedom and life to its members and to all with whom it comes in contact. To be true to her inmost nature, the Church must actively identify itself with what St. Paul referred to as "whatever things are true, whatever honorable, whatever just, whatever lovable, whatever of good repute . . ." (Phil 4:8). In this way it will become before the eyes of all the world what Michael Novak, in the title of a recent book, has called "The Open Church."

But history makes it clear that at various times the Church has tended to take on some of the characteristics of a closed society. It is not surprising that this should be so; for, as Paul VI has reminded us, "the actual image of the Church is never as perfect, as lovely, as holy or as brilliant as that formative divine idea would wish it to be" (*Ecclesiam suam*, n. 11). As members of the race of Adam, we are all subject to tribalism and clannishness; we are instinctively aggressive, proud, suspicious, and contentious. Quite naturally, then, we Christians (and we Catholics not less than others) have often looked upon the Church as a particular group surrounded by competitors, as a closed society which must defend itself against its enemies.

It could, I think, be shown that the traumatic experiences of the Protestant Reformation and the four centuries of ugly conflicts that followed (against deism, rationalism, naturalism, and various brands of atheism) subjected the Church to a particular temptation in this regard. They created an emergency situation in which the Church was practically forced to take on the attributes of a closed society. Wounded by a series of revolts from within and aggressions from without, it became anxious for its own survival and self-defense. It looked on other religious groups with hostility and suspicion. Imitating somewhat the militaristic states of post-Renaissance Europe, the Church became centralized, autocratic, almost imperialistic. Loyalty to the Church was viewed in terms of iron discipline and blind obedience. The apostolate itself was conceived as a spiritual warfare, having as its goal the conquest of souls.

This background provides the key to much of the discussion of the dimensions of the Church in the period from the Counter Reformation to the opening of Vatican II. In reply to certain Protestants, who insisted that the true Church was heavenly and invisible, Catholics stressed almost exclusively the visible elements. The thought of Cardinal Bellarmine dominates the whole period. "The one and true Church," he wrote, "is a group of men bound together by the profession of the same Christian faith and by the communion of the same sacraments, under the rule of the legitimate pastors, and especially of the one vicar of Christ on earth, the Roman pontiff. From this definition it can easily be gathered which men belong to the Church, and which do not." [1] Outside the Church, in Bellarmine's view, are all pagans, Jews, Moslems, heretics, and apostates (in short, all who lack the true faith); likewise all catechumens and excommunicates (since they have no access to the sacraments); and finally all schismatics (since they are not subject to the legitimate pastors). Obviously, on this definition one may meet the requirements for membership without grace or charity. More than this, Bellarmine maintains that a man who is a secret infidel, and who merely makes external pretense of believing, should be reckoned a member; otherwise the visibility of the Church would be compromised. "For the Church is a group of men as visible and palpable as that of the Roman people, or the Kingdom of France, or the Republic of Venice."

The great weakness of Bellarmine's view, as set forth in this passage, is that it omits precisely what makes the Church the Church, namely, the communion of minds and hearts through sharing in the same divine life. Recognizing this weakness, Bellarmine went on to speak of the "soul," as distinct from the "body," of the Church, but in so doing he weakened his previous insistence on the Church's perfect visibility.

Vatican II, in its Constitution on the Church, draws somewhat on the thought of Bellarmine but gets away from his excessive preoccupation with visibility. Instead of looking on the Church as an external society similar to a national state, the Constitution begins with a chapter on

[1] *De controversiis*, Vol. 2, *De conciliis et ecclesia*, Book 3, chap. 2 (Naples: Giuliano, 1875, Vol. 2, 75). In fairness we should add that this one passage from the *Controversies*, stressing the juridical, does not fully express Bellarmine's concept of the Church. Cf. F. Malmberg, S.J., *Eén Lichaam en één Geest* (Utrecht: Spectrum, 1958) pp. 24–25.

"The Mystery of the Church," with the implication that it defies precise definition and escapes the neat pigeonholes of human thought. In his opening allocution at the Second Session (Sept. 29, 1963), Paul VI declared: "The Church is a mystery. It is a reality imbued with the hidden presence of God. It lies, therefore, within the nature of the Church to be always open to new and greater exploration." In entitling this chapter "The Dimensions of the Church," I am by no means proposing to measure the Church, but rather seeking to call attention to its immensity. St. Paul prayed that the Ephesians might be able to comprehend "the breadth and length and height and depth" of the love of Christ—and then immediately added that it "surpasses knowledge" (Eph 3:18 f.). So likewise we may speak in a metaphorical way of the height, depth, breadth, and length of the Church, and seek to comprehend them so far as our capacity allows.

Concerning the height of the Church one may truly say that if its feet are on earth, its head is in heaven. Some theologians since Bellarmine have thought that one could be fully a member of the Church without the vivifying influence of divine grace and that only visible or juridical elements were necessary for incorporation. The Encyclical *Mystici corporis* (1943) broke new ground by its emphasis on the Holy Spirit as soul of the Church. Vatican II followed this up by stating that no one is fully incorporated in the Body unless he has the Holy Spirit, the Spirit of Christ. What is most distinctive of the Church, therefore, is not subject to human verification, but accessible only to the eyes of faith. We might expect as much if the Church is by nature a mystery.

[6]

As this term implies, the Church is an intimate union of the human with the divine. If God had not Himself revealed this union, the very concept would sound almost blasphemous. The Constitution on the Church dares even to compare it with the mystery of the union of the two natures in Jesus Christ. The Church as a visible, hierarchical structure and as a spiritual community of grace is only a single Church, "one interlocked reality which is comprised of a divine and a human element. For this reason, by an excellent analogy, this reality is compared to the mystery of the Incarnate Word" (n. 8).

In chapter 1, the Constitution on the Church reaffirms the essential teaching of *Mystici corporis* on the Church as Christ's mystical Body, animated by His Holy Spirit. Christ, we are told, "fills the Church, which is His Body and His fulness, with His divine gifts, so that she may grow and reach all the fulness of God" (n. 7).

This theme of the splendor of the Church, taken in isolation, might lead us to divinize it excessively, so that we would risk adoring the Church in place of Christ Himself. But the height of the Church must be balanced against its depth, its splendor against its misery. Can we say that the Church as a human institution is unfaithful to its Lord, even that it lapses into sin?

The question calls for distinctions. A man's answer depends on how he is thinking of the Church. Until recently it has been customary to think of the Church in terms of its essential divine principles, as established and sustained by Christ. From this point of view, the Church is entirely exempt from sin and error. *Mystici corporis* adopted this standpoint when it declared that the Church as mother "is spotless in the sacraments, by which she gives birth to her children and nourishes them; she is spotless in the faith which she has preserved inviolate always, in her sacred laws imposed upon all, in the evangelical counsels which she recommends, in those heavenly gifts and extraordinary graces through which, with inexhaustible fecundity, she generates hosts of martyrs, virgins, and confessors. But it cannot be laid to her charge if some members fall weak or wounded." [2]

The theology of Vatican II is, on the whole, concrete and historical rather than abstract and metaphysical. Accordingly the Council prefers to speak of the Church not as the bare essence of "what Christ instituted" but rather as what results when men of flesh and blood gather in such an institution. The concrete image of the People of God dominates the second chapter especially. The Church, concretely considered, can be deeply involved in sin. It is constituted of sinners, so much so that Scripture can tell us: "If we say that we have no sin, we deceive ourselves, and the truth is not in us" (1 Jn 1:8). Avoiding anything that might smack of complacency or triumphalism, Vatican II calls attention to the contrast between Christ and the Church. "While Christ, holy, innocent, undefiled (Heb 7:26), knew nothing of sin (2 Cor 5:21), the Church, embracing sinners in her bosom, is at the same time holy and always in need of being purified, and incessantly pursues the path of penance and renewal" (n. 8).

The Church, then, is not a pure idea existing in some supracelestial realm. It is not a society of saints alone, as the Donatists and other heretics imagined. It is an assemblage of

[2] Pius XII, *Mystici corporis Christi* (*AAS* 35 [1943] 223); Eng. tr., *The Mystical Body of Christ* (America Press ed.) no. 81.

men who always fall short of what God requires of them, and who therefore need forgiveness. The Church, therefore, prays for purification and renewal, as in the Prayer of the Assembly for the 15th Sunday after Pentecost: "Let thy continual pity purify and defend thy Church; and because she cannot continue in safety without thee, direct her always by thy gracious help." The Decree on Ecumenism can even speak of the Church's need of reformation: "Christ summons the Church, as she goes her pilgrim way, to that continual reformation of which she always has need, insofar as she is an institution of men here on earth" (n. 6).

If anyone ignored either the height of the Church, by which it shares in the divine life, or the depth, by which it shares in the life of sinful men, he would have too limited an idea of the Church. However difficult it may be to reconcile these two aspects, we must retain both lest we err by oversimplifying.

Let us now turn to consider the Church, so to speak, horizontally. How wide is it spread here on earth? The question of inclusiveness is a complex one and must be treated piecemeal.

Until Vatican II, most Catholics were content to say that the Church of Christ is the Roman Catholic Church, and that it includes only those who are joined to it by the triple bond of creed, code, and cult specified in Bellarmine's definition. According to this view, no one would be in the Church of Christ unless he professed the Catholic faith, was subject to the Roman pontiff, and had access to the sacraments.

This concept of the Church, inherited from the Counter Reformation, was in substance reaffirmed in a much-discussed paragraph of Pius XII's Encyclical *Mystici corporis*. But this rather monolithic view never won full acceptance. Indeed, it created severe problems for Catholic theology. If the Church was necessary for salvation—as all Catholics held that it must be—then how could there by any hope of salvation for the non-Catholic? Some, following a suggestion in *Mystici corporis*,[3] maintained that non-Catholics could be connected with the Church by at least some kind of implicit desire for membership, but others questioned whether it was correct to rest man's eternal salvation on something purely interior and invisible. If man is a social and corporeal being, how can he be saved in a purely private and spiritual way? In order to be efficacious, his relationship to the Church would seem to demand some kind of corporate, social manifestation.

The problem, how broad the Church is, is far from solved in contemporary theology. But Vatican II, by its surprising refusal to identify the Church of Christ exclusively with Roman Catholicism, has opened up new avenues of thought. In the Constitution on the Church we read that while the Church of Christ does subsist in the Roman Catholic communion, "many elements of sanctification and truth can be found outside her visible structure" (n. 8). This general principle lays the foundation for the doctrine of the "elements of the Church" set forth in the Decree on Ecumenism with reference to Christians of other denominations: "Some, even very many, of the most significant

[3] *Suprema haec sacra* (letter of the Holy Office written to the Archbishop of Boston in 1949, on the occasion of the Leonard Feeney controversy) calls attention to, and spells out in greater detail, this suggestion of *Mystici corporis*; cf. Denzinger-Schönmetzer, *Enchiridion symbolorum* (32nd ed.; Freiburg: Herder, 1963) n. 3871.

elements or endowments which together go to build up and give life to the Church herself can exist outside the visible boundaries of the Catholic Church: the written word of God, the life of grace, faith, hope, and charity, along with other interior gifts of the Holy Spirit and visible elements" —most importantly, the sacraments (n. 3). As we shall see in chapter 2, this line of thought permits a very positive appraisal of the Churches and ecclesial communities separated from Rome.

In the case of non-Catholic Christianity, therefore, we should clearly recognize the presence of churchly realities outside the Catholic Church. These realities can include, in the case of Orthodox Christianity, a validly ordained priesthood and all the seven sacraments. Thus the separate Christian Churches and their members should not be considered as if they were simply separated from Christ, from the Church, and from ourselves. All the authentic Christian elements existing among the various Churches are vital links and sources of spiritual unity.

From the Council's statements about non-Catholic Christianity we may conclude that the Church is not a simple quantity which is either wholly present or wholly absent. Rather, it is something which can be more or less realized, according to the measure in which God's saving work in Christ is believed and lived. This raises the further question, whether anything of the Church can be present where the gospel has not been preached or accepted. This question is obviously of immense significance for the dimensions of the Church. If the answer is no, we shall have to say that the Church is absent from most of the contemporary world, which is only one-third Christian. And yet it sounds farfetched to speak of a presence of the Church among men who do not even recognize Christ as their Saviour.

The Council did not directly discuss the presence of the Church in the non-Christian world. I shall, therefore, rely at this point on the speculations of several modern theologians who seem to me to be in line with the Council, but who deliberately seek to go beyond its express teaching.

Let us begin by considering the role of Christ. In the plan of God, He is the center of the universe. It is in Him that all creation has its full intelligibility. He is the Alpha which stands at the origin of all things, and the Omega—or goal—to which they tend. As we read in the Constitution on the Church in the Modern World: "God's Word, by whom all things were made, was Himself made flesh so that as perfect man He might save all men and sum up all things in Himself. The Lord is the goal of human history, the focal point of the longings of history and civilization, the center of the human race, the joy of every heart, and the answer to all its yearnings" (n. 45).

In contemporary Catholic theology it is taken for granted that the saving grace of Christ is at work among all men, and hence is operative far beyond the limits of the institutional Church. Many theologians speak in this connection of "anonymous Christianity." By this they mean that men who have not heard, or do not consciously accept, the good news of the Christian gospel, and who perhaps do not even think of themselves as believers in God, may nevertheless be living by the grace of Christ when they follow the dictates of their conscience. If we grant the existence of such an "anonymous Christianity," we must further ask how it is related to the Church. Some would say that Christ's activity as risen Lord transcends that of

His Body the Church, and that He is present where the Church has not yet arrived.

But this statement seems to reflect too narrow a view of the Church. I prefer to say with Schillebeeckx that "the acts of Christ in glory are the acts of the whole Christ, the integral Christ in and with his Body the Church." [4] He quotes in this connection the remarkable assertion of the German exegete Heinrich Schlier, commenting on Paul's Letter to the Ephesians: "There is no sphere of being that is not also the Church's sphere. The Church is fundamentally directed to the universe. Her boundaries are those of the universe. There is no realization of Christ's dominion without the Church or beyond her, no 'fulfilment' apart from her. The way in which the universe grows toward Christ is the way the Church grows." [5]

If this is true, we must speak of two distinct ways in which the Church can be present and active. On the one hand, there is an institutional presence of the Church in historical continuity with the ministry of Christ its Founder. This presence implies an explicit profession of the Christian faith as channeled by Scripture and tradition, and normally includes sacramental forms of worship. But short of this, there is an active presence of the Church even among those who have not yet been confronted with the forms of creed and cult historically deriving from Jesus Christ. In this connection we might perhaps speak of an "anonymous Church," corresponding to the anonymous Christianity already mentioned.

How would such an anonymous Church come into

---

[4] E. Schillebeeckx, O.P., "The Church and Mankind," in *Concilium* 1 (New York: Paulist Press, 1965) 87.

[5] *Ibid.*, p. 91.

being? As I have already mentioned, man is neither a pure spirit nor an isolated individual. He is a corporeal and social being. This means that the structure of his religious life, in agreement with the structure of his very being, will inevitably have a visible and communal aspect. Wherever anonymous Christianity is present, some kind of quasi-sacramental visibility will accompany it. In this way, as Schillebeeckx puts it, something of the Mystical Body is brought to visible realization, though only in a veiled manner. We have, as it were, a secret presence of the Church even where the spoken or written word of the gospel has not yet penetrated.

In this perspective we can better appreciate the significance of the non-Christian religions. Whenever men in society express their inner spiritual aspirations and intuitions by word and gesture, religious communities begin to take shape. Through myths and rituals and other symbolic forms the various religions of the world express in manifold ways man's unquenchable thirst for union with the divine, his hope of salvation, his confidence in redemption. These themes are not confined to the biblical religions. In a special way, of course, Christ fulfilled the Israelite religion which providentially prepared the context of His own advent and career. But in a larger sense we can say that He, as the Incarnate Word, crowns all the religions of the world. The doctrinal and cultic life which characterizes these other religions is an adumbration and even an incipient presence of the Church of Christ.

The search for authentic human communion and fulfilment is not confined to organizations which are professedly religious. Men who labor for the building of international peace and brotherhood, or for social justice within any community, may be faithfully following the impulses of a divine and Christian charity. There is no strict line of demarcation between the Church and the world. They are not two spatially distinct societies, but two aspects of a single dynamic complex. Christians are not removed by their membership in the Church from full communion with the human family. Rather, they are that portion of mankind which has come to recognize Christ as Saviour of the world. The Church, therefore, stands where all mankind should be. "In the strict sense," writes Schillebeeckx, "the Church is mankind insofar as it willingly places itself under Christ's influence through faith and baptism, and 'helps its unbelief' at the common table of the eucharist." [6]

So close are the relations between the Church and the world that it seems hardly possible to make a sharp distinction between their goals. If all mankind was created for salvation, and salvation means an authentic fellowship of men in the Body of Christ, the Church really exists to remind the world of its own nature and to help it achieve itself.

The borders between the Church and the world are forever shifting. The world, insofar as it draws near to God in Christ, becomes more and more the Church. And the Church, insofar as it forgets God and falls into idolatry, becomes more and more the world—that world for which Christ would not pray. The aim of pastoral and missionary activity is to diffuse the Church in its full intensity, as broadly as may be, among all men, and in this sense to make the world become the Church. "The Church," as *Lumen gentium* expresses it, "simultaneously prays and labors in order that the entire world may become the People of God,

[6] *Ibid.*, p. 87.

the Body of the Lord, and the Temple of the Holy Spirit, and that in Christ, the Head of all, there may be rendered to the Creator and Father of the universe all honor and glory" (n. 17).

Let us now turn to the final "dimension"—the length of the Church. How long has it existed and how long is it destined to endure? Most Catholics would say that it came into being on Calvary or at Pentecost, and that it will last till the end of the world, since the gates of hell will not prevail against it. This answer would give the Church a respectable duration of some millennia, but it would still fail to do justice to the total importance of the Church in God's plan of creation. When the early Christian writer Hermas, writing in Rome about the end of the first century, described his visions, he reported that the Church appeared to him in the guise of a venerable old woman. "Why is she so elderly?" he asked the angel. "Because," came the reply, "she was created the first of all things. For this reason she is an old woman. And for her sake was the world established" (*Shepherd*, Vision 2, 4, 1). To consider the Church as if the age from Pentecost to the Parousia spanned its entire existence is as faulty as to define a plant as a mere stem without reference to its roots or its flower. We must consider the roots of the Church in its prehistory and its flowering in the posthistorical era that is to come.

As regards the origins of the Church, Vatican II took pains to stress that it did not begin abruptly with the coming of Christ, but that it had a long period of preparation, especially in God's dealings with Israel. In designating the Church as the New Israel and especially as the People of

God, the Council reminds us that the Church would be unintelligible unless seen against the Old Testament background. At several points the Vatican Constitution alludes to the familiar patristic theme of the Church as a reality which in some sort existed from the time of Abel, the just one. This realization that the Church of Christ stands in continuity with the earliest religious aspirations of the race should increase our sense of solidarity with the past and with that great portion of mankind who still stand in a situation comparable to the biblical people before the time of Abraham or Moses.

Even more important for our idea of the Church is a realization of its future destiny. Many Catholics seem to forget that the Church really has a history. They think of it statically as if it were immune from change and incapable of progress. But if we look at the Church concretely and historically, rather than as an abstract essence, we shall see that it has a dramatic life story through the centuries. The picture of the Church as a pilgrim making its way through history is beautifully painted for us by Vatican II: "Moving forward through trial and tribulation, the Church is strengthened by the power of God's grace promised to it by the Lord, so that in the weakness of the flesh it may not waver in perfect fidelity, but remain a bride worthy of the Lord; that moved by the Holy Spirit it may never cease to renew itself, until through the Cross it arrives at the light which knows no setting" (n. 9).

One of the greatest achievements of the Constitution on the Church is to have restored the notion of the Church triumphant. To see the Church in this world as a pilgrim is already to raise the question, what is the goal of this march through the desert? What of the promised land? In chapter

7, inserted at the suggestion of Pope John XXIII, the Vatican Constitution firmly teaches that the Church will fully achieve itself in heaven. Most of us have been far too individualistic in our ideas about the afterlife. We imagine that it will be a private affair between God and ourselves, in which other men, including Christ Himself, will play no vital part. Chapter 7, without saying anything radically new, gives what we may call an ecclesial context to Catholic eschatology. As Fr. Molinari has observed, "It is one of the outstanding merits of this chapter to have offered, for the first time in the history of dogma, a full and organic exposition of our union with the Church in heaven and to have placed it in its proper Christological and ecclesiological setting." [7]

If we view the Church simply as pope, bishops, sacraments, and sermons, we shall find in our thinking no place for the Church triumphant. But we should look upon the Church, above all else, as the communion of saints with one another and, through Christ, with God. Then we shall be able to center our minds and hearts upon the thrilling promise with which chapter 7 concludes: "For when Christ shall appear and the glorious resurrection of the dead takes place, the splendor of God will brighten the heavenly city and the Lamb will be the lamp thereof. Then in the supreme happiness of charity the whole Church of the saints will adore God and 'the Lamb who was slain,' proclaiming with one voice: 'To him who sits upon the throne, and to the Lamb, blessing and honor and glory and dominion, forever and ever" (n. 51).

This eschatological hope should never detract from our

[7] P. Molinari, S.J., *Saints: Their Place in the Church* (New York: Sheed & Ward, 1965) p. 172.

loving concern for this world and its salvation. The gospel forbids us to cultivate a "contempt of the world" in this negative sense. Believers should be willing to spend themselves and be spent in order that the naked may be clothed and the hungry fed. But it would be no less an error to measure everything by its contribution to the city of man. We must never forget that "the form of this world is passing away." Amid all trials and distress the Christian is sustained by an assurance of a final kingdom which will be of God's making, and not man's alone. As the Letter to the Hebrews tells us, "we have not here a lasting city but we look for one that is to come" (13:14). If we keep our hearts where our true treasure is, that is, where Christ is seated at the right hand of the Father, we shall not be lacking in that courage, hope, and enthusiasm which the world has the right to expect from the convinced Christian. We shall have, thanks to our faith, an Archimedes' platform from which to raise the world toward God.

In this age of secular Christianity we need to keep reminding ourselves that man was not made for this life alone. It will do no good to build fairer cities on this earth if we do not at the same time help man find a path toward heaven. St. Augustine gave magnificent expression to the eschatological dimension of our hope and charity when he laid down the rule:

. . . we are to love what can be brought with us into those realms where no one says "my father," but where everyone addresses the one God as "our Father"; where no one says "my mother," but where everyone greets that Jerusalem as "our Mother"; where no one says "my brother," but where everyone refers to everyone else as "our brother". . . .[8]

In a time of widespread suspicion and restlessness it is easy to become impatient with the complexities of the full Christian reality and to find oppositions and conflicts wherever there are tensions and contrasts. To avoid such imbalances, we need to keep our eyes open to the full dimensions of the Church, with all its surprising variety of aspects. It would be fatal to ignore either the institutional Church or the mystical Church, either the pilgrim Church or the triumphant Church, either the human Church or that which is of God. It would be disastrous to divide or separate what God has bound together. The Church is a great mystery, surpassing comprehension, and must therefore be approached with reverence. Its inexhaustible riches provide endless matter for thought and exploration. If anyone feels hemmed in by the Church, he would do well to ask himself whether he has ever caught the vision of the full Church, the universal Church, the Catholic Church.

[8] *The Lord's Sermon on the Mount* 1, 41; tr. D. J. Kavanagh, O.S.A., in *The Fathers of the Church* 11 (New York: Fathers of the Church, 1951) 62.

★ 2 ★

The Church and the Churches

John XXIII, with the clarity characteristic of his genius, recognized that the Catholic Church, in the previous few centuries, had become too much turned in upon itself. Instead of radiating life and holiness to a world which desperately needed such an influence, the Church had become static, isolated, estranged from the world. With remarkable success, Pope John succeeded in reversing this trend in the few short years of his pontificate. The Council was faithful to this intention of the great Pope who conceived and convened it. As we read in the first article of the Constitution on the Church:

The Council wishes to set forth more precisely to the faithful and to the entire world the nature and encompassing mission of the Church. The conditions of this age lend special urgency to the Church's task of bringing all men to full union with Christ, since mankind today is joined more closely together than ever before by social, technical, and cultural bonds.

In chapter 1 we concentrated on what the Church itself is, and saw something of its immensity. It cannot be divorced from the world or from men of any kind and condition. In the next three chapters, probing further into the "breadth" of the Church, I should like to take up various aspects of what Cardinal Suenens, in an important address in the aula of St. Peter's, called the "outgoing Church," *Ecclesia ad extra.* Taking a cue from Paul VI's Encyclical *Ecclesiam suam,* we may divide the outer realms, to which the Church must dynamically relate itself, into three: the other Christian communities, the peoples still to be evangelized, and the world of secular life. These chapters will, therefore, touch on the vital issues of ecumenism, missiology, and Christian secularity. As a basic source for all three chapters I shall use the Dogmatic Constitution on the Church. But in addition I shall draw heavily upon three other documents: for the first topic, the Decree on Ecumenism; for the second, the Decree on Missionary Activity; and for the third, the Pastoral Constitution on the Church in the Modern World.

These questions should be of interest even to persons not concerned in any professional way with the particular subject matter of these chapters; for all these topics are pertinent to the self-understanding of the Church. As members of the Church, we naturally feel ill at ease unless we can see the Church in relation to the rest of created reality. Like the individual person, the Church is in need of external contacts in order to establish its own identity.

The ecumenical problem is not new in our century. In fact, it is as old as Christian dissension—which means, as old as the Church itself. In a sense it even goes back to Old Testament times, when the unity of God's people was torn by the deep rift between Judah and Israel. But for present purposes it will be sufficient to consider the situation which has arisen in the Western world as a result of the Protestant Reformation of the sixteenth century. Luther, Calvin, and the other Protestant founders did not establish a completely new religion. They intended only to reform the Christianity which they knew, and bring it back to its pristine purity. From the "undivided" Church they inherited the Bible, the early creeds and other monuments of ancient tradition, and many sacraments and liturgical forms. They professed the central dogmas of the Trinity and the divinity of Christ in essentially the same terms as Catholic Christians. Hence we have from the beginning an ambivalent situation. Protestants and Catholics anathematized each other in the name of one and the same fundamental Christian faith. The Reformation looked on itself as a return to the original, biblical faith, whereas Catholicism looked on itself as the only custodian of the full revelation of Christ.

The ambivalence of the situation itself opened the way for many fluctuations in Protestant-Catholic relations. Until a century ago official Catholic estimates of the values in Protestant Christianity were almost entirely negative. As long as the two great branches of Western Christianity were in polemical confrontation, Catholics concentrated chiefly on what Protestantism was alleged to lack, e.g., valid orders, a valid Eucharist, and an authoritative magisterium. Although Catholic theologians of this period admitted the validity and efficacy of infant baptisms administered by Protestants, it was seriously doubted whether anyone raised in Protestantism could make a supernatural act of faith. While simple and religiously uneducated Protestants might get into heaven thanks to their baptism, educated Protestants, according to a widely-held view, would inevitably incur eternal damnation unless they formally entered the Catholic Church before they died.

Under the pressure of nineteenth-century Liberalism, Pius IX took cautious steps toward a more optimistic evaluation of the possibilities of salvation open to Christians outside the Catholic fold. In an Encyclical of 1863 he wrote: "Those who are afflicted with invincible ignorance with regard to our holy religion, if they carefully keep the precepts of the natural law that have been written by God in the hearts of all men, if they are prepared to obey God, and if they live a virtuous and dutiful life, can attain to eternal life by the power of divine light and grace." [1] From the standpoint of a century later, we cannot help but be struck with the fact that the Pope apparently looked upon Protestant and Orthodox Christians as being in the same situation as pagans. He makes no mention of the power of God's word as heard by these other Christians, or of their institutional and sacramental life. In its accent on natural law the Encyclical mirrors the prevailing rationalism of the nineteenth century; in the primary place which it accords to subjective sincerity and good will, the emphasis is excessively individualistic.

Pius XII in *Mystici corporis* (1943) and *Suprema haec sacra* (Letter of the Holy Office, 1949) speaks of the salvation of non-Catholics from a more "ecclesial" point of view. To attain eternal life, men must have at least an implicit desire for the Church (*votum ecclesiae*). But this desire, so far as appears from these documents, would seem to be something purely spiritual and internal. Many Orthodox, Anglicans, and Protestants objected to these documents, since they seemed to put non-Roman Christians on the same footing as non-Christians. They gave no ecclesial

---

[1] Encyclical *Quanto conficiamur moerore*, Aug., 1863 (Denzinger-Schönmetzer, n. 2866; Eng. tr. in J. F. Clarkson, S.J., *The Church Teaches* [St. Louis: Herder, 1955] n. 178).

value to any religious communities other than the Catholic Church.

The ecumenical theology of the 1950's prepared the way for Vatican II by developing the doctrine of *vestigia ecclesiae* (traces of the Church). The fundamental idea behind this doctrine goes back to the anti-Donatist writings of St. Augustine; it was further developed by Luther and Calvin in their remarks about the Catholic Church, which they considered to be a defective realization of Christianity. In modern Catholic teachings the idea was strikingly expressed by Pius XI in 1927: "Detached fragments of a gold-bearing rock also contain the precious ore. The ancient Churches of the East have retained so true a holiness that they deserve not only our respect but also our sympathy." [2] A number of Catholic theologians in the 1950's applied these principles to the Protestant Churches, in which they found many elements of sanctification taken from the Catholic Church. These elements, although belonging by right to Catholicism, were truly effective among other Christians; they were powerful links with the ancient Church and made that Church in some sort dynamically present among these other communions.

The doctrine of *vestigia ecclesiae* marked a notable advance over previous efforts to explain the possibilities of salvation for non-Catholic Christians in terms of their subjective good faith. But it failed to do justice to the continuing vitality of these other communions. The term *vestigia* seemed to suggest deterioration; it did not sufficiently allow for the renewing breath of the Holy Spirit. Nor did the doctrine of *vestigia* give any positive and distinctive value to communities outside of Roman Catholicism. It suggested

[2] French translation and comment in *Irénikon* 3 (1927) 20.

that they could be adequately assessed in terms of how much they had preserved of the heritage of Catholicism. In the last analysis it gave no ecclesial significance to the other communities as such; grace and salvation were ascribed to the survival of Catholic elements in these communities. Some of the shortcomings of the *vestigia* doctrine still linger in the Decree on Ecumenism of Vatican II; but on the whole, as we shall now see, it represents a new stage in Catholic ecumenical thinking.

We may profitably examine the ecumenical contributions of Vatican II under three headings. First, what does the Council say about Catholic Christianity? Secondly, what does it say about the rest of Christianity? Thirdly, what does it say about the interrelationships between the two? Since the first two questions have to do with ecclesiology rather than with ecumenical action, we may draw our answers as much from the Constitution on the Church as from the Decree on Ecumenism. The two documents in this respect form a single unit and must be read in the light of each other.

The image of the Catholic Church set forth in these documents makes a major ecumenical contribution. For one thing, the ecclesiology is far more flexible than that found in previous official documents. Even *Mystici corporis*, which did a great deal to call attention to the charismatic and mystical dimensions of the Church, was dominated by a rather static and monolithic view. The Church consisted of members, and membership was defined in a way that made it a matter of a simple either/or. If one did not accept the entire institutional framework of the Catholic Church, with its dogmas, sacraments, and hierarchical structure, one was simply not a member.

Vatican II does not reject the teaching of *Mystici corporis*, but as the decisive notion it uses communion or some equivalent (e.g., conjunction, incorporation) rather than membership. Communion is not a matter of either/or; it admits of many levels and degrees of intensity. A man may be in communion with the Church in one respect but not in another. Thus, according to the Decree on Ecumenism, those "who believe in Christ and have been properly baptized are brought into a certain, though imperfect, communion with the Catholic Church" (n. 3). Furthermore, whereas membership, as described in *Mystici corporis*, was something of the external, visible order, incorporation, as set forth in *Lumen gentium*, is primarily constituted by the interior gift of the Holy Spirit, which is sufficient and necessary for salvation (n. 14). This complex and flexible presentation of the various ways in which one can be related to the Church makes room for a far more optimistic view of the ecclesiological position of non-Catholic Christians. They can share in the blessings of the Church without being fully incorporated in the juridical sense.

The Church, considered in its visible or institutional reality, is compared to the sacraments. Just as a sacrament is a sign of the grace which it brings about, so the Church, rather than containing the totality of salvation, points toward it, and strives by its prayers and labors to actualize God's kingdom among men. The salutary influence of the Church radiates far beyond its visible, quasi-sacramental presence. And yet the Church is somehow present wherever the Holy Spirit is at work. According to the famous dictum of St. Irenaeus, "Where the Church is, there too is the Spirit of God; and where the Spirit of God is, there is the Church and every grace." [3] Because the salvific reality which the Church strives to bring into being is of greater importance than the visible token of its presence, there can be a real and very significant followship in grace among persons who are not fully united in the external, institutional aspects of their religious life. The recognition of this fellowship is of the greatest ecumenical importance.

These reflections do not point the way to confessional indifferentism. The Vatican documents make it clear that the Church of Christ subsists in its institutional purity and completeness in the Roman Catholic Church, and nowhere else. Thanks to the efficacious promise of Christ, the churches in full communion with the Petrine See will always possess the objective elements of the total Christian patrimony: the saving doctrine of the gospel, the seven sacraments, and a legitimately empowered ministry.

These objective endowments are signal blessings, but by themselves they do not guarantee the perfection of Christian life. Personal holiness is never achieved without faithful co-operation on the part of the individual with the graces given to him. To whom much is given, of him much shall be required.

Because of this human, personal factor in all Christian life, the Catholic Church, like any other religious body, is in constant need of purification and renewal. Reformation, therefore, is not the prerogative of Protestant Christianity. Catholics too may apply to themselves the truth contained in the classical Protestant slogan *ecclesia semper reformanda*. Such is the clear teaching of the Decree on Ecumenism (n. 6), already quoted in chapter 1: "Christ summons the Church, as she goes her pilgrim way, to that

[3] *Against Heresies* 3, 24, 1 (*Patrologia graeca* 7, 966).

continual reformation of which she always has need, inso-far as she is an institution of men here on earth."

The Second Assembly of the World Council of Churches (Evanston, 1954), in its majority statement on Church Unity, applied to the Church the Lutheran formula "at once righteous and sinful" (*simul iustus et peccator*). And now the Vatican II Constitution on the Church, from a Catholic point of view, has said practically the same thing (n. 8): "The Church, embracing sinners in her bosom, is at the same time holy and always in need of being purified, and incessantly pursues the path of penance and renewal" (n. 8). Among the offenses for which the Church may do penance we find mentioned in the Decree on Ecumenism these sins which have occasioned and perpetuated Christian dissension. "Thus in humble prayer we beg pardon of God and of our separated brethren, just as we forgive them that trespass against us" (n. 7). It is unnecessary to emphasize the enormous contribution made by statements such as these to the possibility of true Christian dialogue with the separated brethren.

The call for purification and reform might be under-stood in the sense of returning to an earlier condition in which Christianity was more perfectly practiced. But the emphasis of Vatican II is not upon return to the past. One of the most remarkable features of the two documents be-fore us is their insistence on the involvement of the pilgrim Church in history. The mutable elements in the Church, such as its liturgy, its canon law, and even the manner in which its doctrinal teaching is formulated, must be con-stantly adapted to the needs and opportunities of the times. Until the pontificate of John XXIII the usual Catholic view was that the Church was somehow immune from the flux of historical process. Whatever development took place was assumed to be linear and homogeneous. But this non-historical view has been discarded by Vatican II. The Church's pilgrimage follows a tortuous route; it struggles against internal weaknesses and external afflictions, and counts upon new outpourings of the Holy Spirit. This more dynamic view of the Church, accenting its human fallibility and its dependence on new inspirations, paves the way for an entirely new relationship to the other Christian communities as fellow wayfarers toward a kingdom which still lies ahead.

Let us now turn to the teaching of the Council concerning these other Christian bodies. The first thing to be noted is that the Catholic Church refrains from claiming to be without qualification identical with the Church of Christ. The Constitution affirms that that Church "subsists in" Roman Catholicism, but deliberately leaves room for the view that something of the Church survives also in other Christian communities. Among the objective elements which may be found beyond the borders of Roman Catholicism the Decree on Ecumenism mentions, for example, baptism, the Bible, Christian prayer, and liturgy. The fact that these gifts of Christ are preserved and administered outside Roman Catholicism gives the other Christian bodies a salutary value, so that they may rightly be called churches or ecclesial communities. In terms of objective elements, there is a vast difference between some of the Eastern Churches, which accept practically the whole Catholic heritage except for the Roman primacy of juris-diction, and some Protestant communities, which acknowl-edge only one or two of the sacraments and profess a rather vague biblicism unsupported by firm dogmatic teaching. In this respect the Decree on Ecumenism seems to suggest that non-Catholic bodies are to be ranged along a sliding scale, according to the extent to which they have preserved the full Catholic patrimony. But this is only one way of looking at the matter. A fuller consideration, as we shall presently see, demands that attention be paid to other aspects.

Do the separated communities deserve to be called churches? For some time, the contention that Christ founded only one Church and that this is identical with Roman Catholicism has been a staple of Catholic apologetics. But it does not seem necessary to deny that man's sinfulness has brought about a certain fragmentation in Christ's heritage. The fact that this fragmentation is contrary to the will of Christ does not prove that the divided communities can never be called "churches."

As Congar pointed out some thirty years ago, the documents of the Roman magisterium have regularly referred to the Eastern communities as churches. This is theologically justified, because it has always been recognized that the universal Church is made up of local churches, each under the presidency of its own bishop. When communion is maintained, these churches are bound together in union with the Petrine See, the center of unity. But what happens in case communion is ruptured? So long as there is valid episcopal succession, the local church continues to exist, but in a state of estrangement from the hub of unity. When reconciliation occurs, there is no need to establish the member church for the first time; this church merely passes from its state of separation to one of full ecclesiastical communion.

The Decree on Ecumenism follows the traditional

practice of the Holy See in calling the separated Eastern communities "churches." But it makes a significant innovation in its way of speaking of the Western communities. It calls them "churches and ecclesial communities of the West." This term implies, first of all, that there are separated churches in the West outside the Orthodox tradition. The Decree does not indicate how many such bodies are "churches," except that the official *Relatio* gives as an example the Old Catholics—a group generally recognized as having valid episcopal orders and hence a valid Eucharist. But one may still ask whether the term "churches" may be used more widely, and yet in a properly theological sense, to include Anglicans, Lutherans, Presbyterians, etc. Without definitively settling this complicated question, paragraph 22 suggests a negative answer, since it uses the expression "ecclesial communities" to designate groups which lack the sacraments of orders and Eucharist.

"Ecclesial community" is a new coinage never used in official Roman documents until the Decree on Ecumenism. The Constitution on the Church used the phrase "churches or ecclesiastical communities," but this phrase, according to Fr. Thomas Stransky,[4] smacked too much of the juridical to satisfy the authors of *De oecumenismo*. The term "ecclesial" in modern theological writing has reference to communities rather than to their official organs.

The distinction between churches and ecclesial bodies, and the various enumerations of the bonds which link some churches more closely than others with Rome, suggest, as we have said, a sliding scale. But it would be unfair, and contrary to the full mind of the Council, to imagine that the separated Christian bodies could be evaluated simply in

[4] *The Decree on Ecumenism* (Glen Rock, N.J.: Paulist Press, 1965) p. 68.

terms of the institutional elements they have retained. They differ vastly from one another in the vigor of their devotional life and in their ability to achieve positive Christian insights demanded by the changing times and situations. Fr. Gregory Baum, in an important article,[5] points out that while the non-Roman bodies are institutionally imperfect realizations of the Church, they may on occasion achieve a level of actual Christian living superior to a given church which is in communion with Rome:

Seen from the viewpoint of the divine institution, the Catholic Church is the one Church of Christ on earth and the other Churches are, in varying degrees, imperfect or defective realizations of this; but seen from the viewpoint of God's merciful and sovereign action, which uses institutional elements but is never dependent on or limited by them, a Christian community is more truly Church when it is more transformed into the People of God, into his family, and into a spiritual brotherhood of faith and charity.

On the basis of the preceding analysis of the ecclesiological status of Catholic and separated Christian bodies, we may turn to the question of their interrelationships. The first and most obvious of these is a relationship of mutual confrontation. From the sixteenth century until almost our own day, the confrontation took the form almost exclusively of controversy—sometimes more polemical, sometimes more irenic. Controversy had as its aim to prove that one's own church is right, the other wrong.

In the twentieth century, thanks to the ecumenical

[5] Gregory Baum, O.S.A., "The Ecclesial Reality of the Other Churches," in *Concilium* 4 (Glen Rock, N.J.: Paulist Press, 1965) 62–86, esp. p. 82.

[33]

movement, the prevalent form of encounter is one of dialogue—a form of discussion based on mutual respect and
presupposing mutual readiness to learn from the other. The
parties to the dialogue are not so much adversaries as partners—partners in a process of getting to know and understand each other, taking advantage of each other's insights,
and seeking together for a better understanding of matters
on which neither side is satisfied that it has the whole
truth.

The Decree on Ecumenism teaches explicitly that
theology is no longer to be studied and set forth in a
polemical manner, as though it were proper to present
other churches at their worst in order to refute them more
easily. On the contrary, efforts should be made to learn
accurately and sympathetically the history, spiritual and
liturgical life, and religious psychology of the separated
brethren (n. 9). Catholics are to take care to present their
own positions in a manner which will in no way become an
obstacle to dialogue. In investigating the central Christian
mysteries, theologians of the several confessions should do
so with humility, charity, and deep reverence for truth, so
that all will be incited "to a deeper realization and a clearer
expression of the unfathomable riches of Christ" (n. 11).

Catholics entering into the ecumenical dialogue have
often been hampered by the feeling that if the fulness of
Christ's patrimony survives in Catholicism, and the other
communions are more or less defective, Catholics really
have nothing to learn from the encounter. They can, of
course, explain their own position and seek to show why it
is reasonable, but to do so is to engage in controversy
rather than in genuine dialogue. In reply we must say on
the basis of the ecumenical ecclesiology of Vatican II that

Catholics may have a great deal to learn from the separated brethren. For one thing, we have seen that the Church, as it empirically exists, is always in need of purification, renewal, and adaptation to the times. The other Christian communities, insofar as they too seek to be faithful to the gospel in the conditions of today's world, may be able to offer welcome criticism and advice. It would be unwarranted to assume that the special traditions of the various Orthodox and Protestant communities have no positive Christian values not already realized in Roman Catholicism. Catholics of a given time and place may be quite deficient in their actual realization of what the gospel implies. And the other Christian bodies, enjoying the grace and assistance of the Holy Spirit, may achieve formulations and adaptations of the Christian message which Catholics would do well to appropriate. Although the Reformers unquestionably erred on certain points, not everything that they said was error. They had some very valid criticisms of what passed for Catholicism in their day and achieved many creative insights into the biblical message.

As has frequently been pointed out, Vatican II adopted a number of positions which had been enunciated by the Reformation Churches, e.g., the primacy of Scripture, the supernatural efficacy of the preached word, the priesthood of the laity, and the vernacular liturgy. The Decree on Ecumenism is rather restrained in acknowledging the indebtedness of the Catholic Church to the Protestant tradition, although it praises the Protestants for their devotion to the Bible, their biblical scholarship, their Christocentric faith, and their readiness to apply the principles of the gospel to moral and social life. In discussing the separated Churches of the East, the Decree shows the highest regard for their spiritual and liturgical traditions. Their theological traditions, moreover, are said to be in many cases complementary rather than opposed to those of the Latin West, and hence worthy of sympathetic study. It is of great importance for Catholicism to regain contact with these elements in its own heritage which have flowered better in the separated churches. As a result of the divisions among Christians, says the Decree (n. 4), "the Church herself finds it more difficult to express in actual life her full catholicity in all its aspects."

Besides these relationships in which Catholic and non-Catholic Christians confront one another vis-à-vis, there are other relationships in which they find themselves side by side, whether before God or before the world. Before God all Christians alike stand in an attitude of worship. Can they pray and worship in common? Until recently, *communicatio in sacris* (common worship) was regarded as being, almost by definition, a sin. But since Vatican II it must be held that in view of the large measure of fellowship among separated Christians, not all common prayer and worship are prohibited. When Christians come together to praise God and implore His blessings, their external worship must be an honest sign.[6] It should neither fail to manifest that measure of unity which truly exists nor imply a closer unity than has been achieved. Otherwise it would be a false sign. In general, the separation among the confessions is unfavorable to common worship; but as the Decree wisely notes (n. 8), the grace to be obtained sometimes commends it. "The concrete course to be adopted, when due regard

---

[6] I borrow this expression from Stransky, *op. cit.*, p. 41.

has been given to all the circumstances of time, place, and persons, is left to the prudent decision of the local episcopal authority, unless the Bishops' Conference, according to its own statutes, or the Holy See has determined otherwise."

Regarding the Holy Eucharist (obviously the most sensitive point in common worship), the Decree on Ecumenism (n. 15) says that since the Eastern Churches preserve apostolic succession in the priesthood and a true Eucharist, some common worship may be permitted by Church authorities. This is affirmed once again, even more emphatically, in the Decree on the Eastern Catholic Churches (nn. 26-29), though it is here added that such Eucharistic intercommunion should not be put into practice unilaterally, without consideration of the desires of the separated Eastern communities, as expressed through their ordinaries.

In the case of religious bodies whose priestly ordinations are not judged valid by the Catholic Church, Eucharistic intercommunion is far more difficult to justify and is definitely not encouraged by the general practice of the Catholic Church. But perhaps, as ecumenical theologians continue to grapple with this difficult question, it may prove possible to find solutions which will somewhat alleviate the hardships of the present situation. In the meanwhile we must patiently accept a measure of painful separation as the penalty for the Christian disunion which we have inherited.

The separated Christians stand together to some extent not only before God but before the world. The Decree, therefore, points out the desirability that they should find ways of confessing together their common faith in the triune God and in the incarnate Son of God, our Redeemer and Lord. All Christians may likewise bear witness to their common hope, which does not play us false (n. 12). It is even a matter of some urgency that we should do so. In the past great harm has been done to the gospel itself by the spectacle of Christian dissensions. In order that the world may believe, it is imperative to manifest that partial unity which we do possess in God and in Christ, and that mutual charity to which all Christians are alike bound by virtue of the gospel to which they all adhere. Christians can ill afford to appear before the world as rivals or enemies.

Closely related to joint witness is common action—a field which corresponds approximately with what in the ecumenical movement has gone by the name of "Life and Work." The Decree on Ecumenism (n. 12) calls for co-operation among Christians in matters such as peace work, the promotion of the arts and sciences, and the relief of social evils such as poverty, hunger, illiteracy, sickness, and inadequate housing. As the Decree reminds us, activities of this sort powerfully set before men's eyes the image of Christ the Servant.

Ecumenism in the order of practical affairs has many other advantages. For one thing, it forges bonds of union among persons who have no special interest or competence in speculative theological questions, or who, if they met on doctrinal matters, would violently anathematize each other. There is more than a grain of truth in the slogan attributed to the Swedish ecumenical pioneer Nathan Söderblom: "Doctrine divides, service unites."

Common action in the social and cultural spheres provides excellent opportunities for Christians to co-operate not only with one another but also with members of other faiths and even with those who subscribe to no definite religious creed. In this way a road is opened to a wider ecumenism, not restricted to those who explicitly accept Christian doctrines.

Within the past year or so a number of observers have been calling for a more secular brand of ecumenism which would place greater emphasis on common service in building up the city of man. This would not be a substitute for, but a necessary complement to, the somewhat churchly type of ecumenism with which we have grown familiar in recent decades. It seems to be true that discussions of faith and church order, unless closely related to problems of life and action, can easily become sterile and academic.

In order to conclude these remarks on the ecumenical significance of the Constitution on the Church and the Decree on Ecumenism, we may squarely put the question, whether they represent a real step forward. A few critics have said that they manifest no basic shift in Roman Catholic ecclesiology, but this reaction is not typical. Most commentaries, from within and without the Catholic communion, have praised these documents, and especially the Decree on Ecumenism, for being clear, concise, persuasive, prudent, and progressive. The main criticism voiced by Protestants and Orthodox is that the Decree is too exclusively based on Catholic ecclesiological positions. Rome is regarded as the norm and center; the other churches are evaluated, at least primarily, in terms of how much they preserve of the Catholic substance, which subsists in its entirety in the Roman communion.[7]

[7] Such is, in substance, the objection of Jean Bosc, quoted by M. Villain, S.M., in his informative article "The Debate on the Decree on Ecumenism," in *Concilium* 14 (Glen Rock, N.J.: Paulist Press, 1966) 128.

Should the Catholic Church plead guilty to this charge and recognize that this is at least a flaw in the Decree? If the charge means that the Catholic Church should disguise or surrender its claim to have preserved the essential fulness of the patrimony conferred by Christ on His Church, the demand would be unreasonable. According to Catholic faith, Christ Himself has guaranteed that this heritage would never be lost. Thus the ultimate unity of Christians, as the Catholic understands it, will necessarily involve a sharing by other churches in the essential form of unity presently existing in the communities in union with Rome.

But the Decree on Ecumenism takes pains to stress that unity does not imply uniformity, and that there is room for an enormous variety of rites and procedures within the Catholic family.

The decisive center of unity and the abiding norm of Christian renewal, according to the Decree, is not the Church in its present empirical form, but rather Christ Himself. All Christians, including Catholics, are summoned to examine their own faithfulness to Christ's will for His Church (n. 6). Since Christ rather than the Church is the underlying source of unity, the Catholic can find a common point of view with any sincere Christian. Beyond the rather stringent unity in doctrine and discipline within the Catholic fold, there is a very significant larger circle of unity embracing all Christians and permitting them to be called, in a memorable phrase of John XXIII, "the whole mystical flock of our Lord."

Christ has bestowed upon this "mystical flock" an effective dynamic principle of unity in the pouring forth of the

---

Similar reservations are expressed by Lukas Vischer in *The Ecumenist* 4, no. 3 (March–April, 1966) 38.

Holy Spirit. The Spirit is not the exclusive possession of any particular body, not even the Catholic Church. He breathes where He wills, and in our day He has been pleased to stir up throughout the Christian world the refreshing breeze of the ecumenical movement. This movement, which began outside the Catholic Church, is a single spiritual thrust making itself felt in practically every Christian group. In acknowledging these facts, the Decree on Ecumenism, not content to look on the Catholic Church as the sole source and measure of all truth and goodness, rejoices in the existence of a larger community of prayer, faith, witness, and endeavor which, though still far from perfect, inspires great hope for the future.

The ultimate unity of Christians, according to the Decree, is not to be conceived of as a simple movement of return of the straying sheep to the one fold of Roman Catholicism, but rather as a bold journey into God's future under the leading of the Holy Spirit. Recognizing that such unity transcends anything that men can produce, the Council puts its reliance on the renewing action of the Holy Spirit, and bids the sons of the Catholic Church to go forward in unison with the separated brethren, without obstructing the ways of divine Providence and without prejudging the future inspirations of heaven. This openness to the unpredictable action of the Spirit, so movingly expressed in the final paragraph of the Decree, provides the strongest basis for confidence in the future of the ecumenical movement.

★ 3 ★

The Church and the Nations

It seems safe to say that the Church's missionary activity, like almost all its other activities, is at present in a state of crisis. By a crisis I do not mean a sudden collapse (like a stock market crisis) but a turning point involving great and decisive changes. The forcible closing of many prosperous missions by hostile political powers, the anti-Western nationalism of many newly independent nations, and the relatively slow rate of conversion of the unevangelized world have convinced some observers that the great day of missionary expansion is past. Some are even asking whether apostolic zeal should not be turned rather to walling up the leakage from the Church on the home front, or to improving the Church's relations with other Christians and with the non-Christian religions. The recent surge of ecumenism and respectful dialogue has made some Christians look on convert-making as unwelcome trespassing. Missionary activity evokes in many minds the image of an aggressive, triumphal Church, an alliance between throne and altar, and a smug Victorian complacency regarding "the white man's burden."

In addition to these difficulties stemming from the historical situation in which we live, there are grave problems of a theoretical order. The relatively new science of missiology has not thus far achieved any widespread consensus as to the nature and purposes of missions. The older assumption that the missionary saves souls by bringing them one by one into the sole ark of salvation has been rapidly losing credit. But no alternative theory has as yet won general popularity. Nor is there any agreement as to what are the proper areas of missionary activity. Some restrict the concept to what used to be called "foreign missions," i.e., journeys to regions where the Church has never yet been planted; others include all forms of evangelization, even in Christian or dechristianized parts of the world; and still others would include under the heading of missions the endeavor to bring separated Christians into the Catholic fold.

A third group of problems revolves around the distribution of missionary tasks within the Church. Are the missions the direct responsibility of all the faithful, or all the hierarchy, or of the pope alone? In view of the principle of collegiality, recently accepted by Vatican II, should the role of the Roman Congregations be reduced? What are the respective powers and responsibility of pope and bishops, of religious orders and diocesan priests, of clergy and laity?

In view of all these problems, it was necessary for Vatican II to treat the question of missions at some length. Dissatisfied with the bare list of fourteen propositions which the co-ordinating commission had proposed in May, 1964, the Council Fathers insisted on a special document dealing with the Church's missionary activity. The Decree *Ad gentes*, adopted at the last session (fall, 1965), does not aim to solve all disputed questions, but it provides valuable guidance regarding many of the more pressing theoretical and practical issues. For anyone seeking the official position of the Church today regarding the missions, a careful study of this document is indispensable.

But in the judgment of history it may well turn out that the most significant advances in missionary doctrine are to be found less in the Decree *Ad gentes* than in the Dogmatic Constitution on the Church, which is from first to last impregnated with missionary concern. This orientation is indicated by the first words of the document, which give it its title, *Lumen gentium:* "Christ is the light of all nations. Hence this most sacred Synod, which has been gathered in the Holy Spirit, eagerly desires to shed on all men that radiance of His which brightens the countenance of the Church. This it will do by proclaiming the gospel to every creature." The fundamental ecclesiological positions set forth in *Lumen gentium* are essential background for understanding the more detailed and practical provisions of the Decree *Ad gentes*. I shall, therefore, draw chiefly on the former document.

While there are many ways of designating what is new in the ecclesiology of Vatican II, it would not be too reckless to say that it marks a shift from a static to a dynamic vision of the Church. For some centuries now the Church has commonly been pictured as a "perfect society" which lacked nothing to make it self-sufficient and complete. While others are invited or even obliged to come in, the Church itself stands firm. Missionaries are like scouts who go out from the Church to urge others to join up. The guests have to travel; the manor house remains where it is.

The Constitution on the Church does not discard all static images of the Church, but the dominant idea is dynamic. The Church is viewed primarily as the new People of God—a people still on the march through the desert, pressing forward through trial and tribulation to the promised land. Interest is focused more than formerly on the external relations of the Church, and consequently too on its relations to the peoples to whom it must communicate the good news of the gospel. In this view missionary activity is not a kind of supererogatory function by which certain individuals venture forth beyond the Church's limits. Rather the Church is missionary by essence. It is, so to speak, a great missionary society; its primary vocation is to be a herald. Constantly in motion, it must deliver its message wherever men are. This vision has been strikingly expressed by the Protestant missiologist J. C. Hoekendijk, who says that the Church in the totality of her being "becomes mission, she becomes the living outreach of God to the world." [1]

In the opening chapter of *Lumen gentium* this missionary role of the Church is theologically derived from the divine missions of the Second and Third Persons of the Blessed Trinity. Article 3 tells us that the Son "came on a mission from His Father"—a mission to establish the kingdom of heaven upon earth. His immediate disciples were called "apostles" (a term meaning missionaries), and He Himself compared their mission to His own: "As the Father has sent me, I send you" (Jn 20:21; cf. *Lumen gentium*, n. 18b). The Church perpetuates this mission, for as we read in article 5, "The Church . . . receives the mission to proclaim and to establish among all peoples the kingdom of Christ and of God." Discountenancing the opinion that the

[1] *The Church Inside Out* (Philadelphia: Westminster Press, 1964) p. 43.

Church actually is the kingdom of God (a static notion), the Council holds that the kingdom is that which the Church must proclaim and inaugurate, and toward the consummation of which it incessantly aspires (n. 9d).

From another point of view, the missionary impetus of the Church is a participation in the mission of the Holy Spirit. Article 4 explains how the Spirit was sent on the day of Pentecost in order to sanctify the Church as a fountain of water springing up to life eternal. The Spirit in the Church is a principle of life and growth, perpetually renewing the Church and stirring up charismatic leaders among both hierarchy and faithful.

The missionary vocation of the Church is intimately connected with that property traditionally called "catholicity." Until a few years ago it was customary to explain this, at least primarily, in quantitative and static terms, i.e., as consisting in the actual spread of the Church to all parts of the globe and in the great multitude of its believers. Contemporary theology adopts a more dynamic and qualitative view of catholicity, founded in the Church's spiritual power to overcome every kind of particularism, cultural, social, geographic, or other. As expressed in *Lumen gentium*, the Church may at times appear to be a "little flock," but its outward thrust is never halted. Transcending all limits of time and of race, "the Church is destined to extend to all regions of the earth and so to enter into the history of mankind" (n. 9g). As stated at the end of chapter 2, "The Church simultaneously prays and labors in order that the entire world may become the People of God, the Body of the Lord, and the Temple of the Holy Spirit" (n. 17c).

Granting the existence of this dynamic thrust, one may

still ask, why the missions? As I have already intimated, it would be naive to hold that missions have as their primary goal the saving of individual souls by bringing them into the safe shelter of the Church. It is, of course, true that a man may be obliged under pain of losing his soul to enter the Church. This point is explicitly made in *Lumen gentium* (n. 14) and quoted verbatim in the document on the missions. But *Lumen gentium* also says quite plainly that those who are inculpably ignorant of the necessity of the Church may be saved without formally entering it. "Those also can attain to everlasting salvation who through no fault of their own do not know the gospel of Christ or His Church, yet sincerely seek God, and, moved by His grace, strive by their deeds to do His will as it is known to them through the dictates of conscience" (n. 16). And the following sentence extends this principle to those who in good faith doubt or deny the existence of God. Such men may be in a hidden way living by the grace of God and of Christ. Because of this real but unrecognized relationship to Christ as their Redeemer, modern theologians sometimes speak in this connection of "latent" (Tillich) or "anonymous" (Rahner) Christians or "unconscious Christianity" (Bonhoeffer).

Once the existence of anonymous Christianity is admitted, it becomes more difficult to show why the Church must carry on missionary activity in every land. The facts that Christ has lived and that His Church is established somewhere might seem sufficient to serve as a channel of salutary grace to the unevangelized, wherever they may be.

As an answer to our problem, some would point out that men who have not been enlightened by the gospel are in greater danger of falling into unbelief and idolatry, thus losing their souls. This seems to be supported by a statement in *Lumen gentium* (n. 16d):

> Rather often men deceived by the Evil One have become caught up in futile reasoning and have exchanged the truth of God for a lie, serving the creature rather than the Creator [cf. Rom 1:21, 25]. Or there are some who, living and dying in a world without God, are subject to utter hopelessness. Consequently, to promote the glory of God and procure the salvation of such men ... the Church painstakingly fosters her missionary work.

The Decree on Missionary Activity amplifies this explanation of why non-Christians stand in need of the gospel. The saving doctrine of Christ is needed to free individuals and societies from sin and servitude, and likewise to manifest to men in every situation "the real truth about their condition and their total vocation" (n. 8).

All these reasons are powerful incentives for missionary activity in the wide sense of bringing the tidings of Christian redemption to as many people as possible. But it must be noted that missionary work, as understood in the Decree *Ad gentes,* is a somewhat narrower term. Its specific purpose is described as "evangelization and the planting of the Church among those persons and groups where the Church has not yet taken root" (n. 6). The expression "planting the Church," which has loomed large in the missiological literature of the past generation, requires a word of explanation. On the one hand, it excludes a purely actualistic view, which would maintain that the Church, having no stable existence, comes into existence each time the gospel is announced or confessed. On the other hand, it respects the vital mystery of the Church. To plant the Church is to sow the seed of the gospel and to provide the conditions for its growth; but God alone gives the increase (cf. 1 Cor 3:6). Thus the planting of the Church should not be misunderstood as though it meant primarily the erecting of churchly buildings or the establishment of an indigenous hierarchy.

In some sense the planting of the Church is never complete, because the Church does not continue automatically in existence where it has once been planted. Sometimes areas which have been evangelized must be evangelized once again because they have become dechristianized. We may well find that, in view of the increasing "diaspora situation" of the Church in the modern world, the distinction between mission lands and other areas will become so narrow as to be no longer significant. But at the present time there is an important difference between the countries where Christianity is widely known and accepted, and those where it has yet to make an impression. The Decree on the Missionary Activity of the Church, without drawing rigid lines between missionary and other areas, endorses this distinction.[2]

In asking about the missions, therefore, we are raising the question why the Church should evangelize new areas rather than devote its entire energies to improving the condition of Christianity in lands where the Church has already taken root. If the goal were simply to give Christian faith to those who lacked it, a good case might be made for bringing most of our missionaries home and setting them to work in the local neighborhood, where they might find it easier to get into effective contact with the people and where, in our day, they would find no lack of unbelief.

[2] For a more precise and nuanced statement on the notion of missionary activity, the reader is referred to *Ad gentes*, n. 6, with the official footnotes.

To show the necessity of going abroad, some would appeal to the command of Christ that the gospel should be announced to all the nations. The missionary mandate of the risen Lord is recorded in various forms in all four Gospels and in Acts 1:8, and all these passages are cited in *Lumen gentium* and in *Ad gentes*. These texts sufficiently establish that missionary activity is required, but they do not explain the reason for it. Presumably, if Christ demanded such a strenuous effort, there must be some real value to be achieved through missionary work.

Again, it helps little to say that God is glorified through the missions; for presumably He would not be glorified unless man were somehow benefited by this labor, according to the famous dictum of Irenaeus, "God's glory is man alive" (*gloria Dei vivens homo*).

No doubt it is also true, as we have suggested above, that the interior movement of the Holy Spirit impels committed Christians to seek, so far as in them lies, to spread their faith. Enthusiastic devotees of almost any cause may well feel compelled to proclaim their convictions, and their words and gestures will be a living proof of the intensity of their commitment. This analogy helps to account for missionary activity, but by itself it fails to show why such activity is useful for the salvation of the world. Yet the Council indicates that there is some connection. After quoting the Pauline text "Woe to me, if I do not preach the gospel" (1 Cor 9:16), the Constitution goes on to say: "The Church is compelled by the Holy Spirit to do her part toward the full realization of the will of God, who has established Christ as the source of salvation for the whole world" (n. 17b).

The best clue to the salvific value of missionary work

lies, I believe, in the statement made several times in *Lumen gentium* that the Church is the "universal sacrament of salvation" (n. 48b). From general sacramental theology we know that a sacrament is an efficacious sign of grace permanently instituted by Christ. Like the seven sacramental rites, the Church itself, as a kind of general sacrament, was evidently instituted by Christ to be an enduring means of salvation. Article 1, moreover, shows a still closer analogy by pointing out that the Church, like the particular sacraments, is at once a sign and an instrument of salvation. This suggests that the Church must signify what it accomplishes, namely, the salvation of the nations.

Christ Himself is, of course, the primordial sign of God's will to redeem mankind. His words, His miracles, and the whole form of His life symbolically express His salvific mission. But the logic of the Incarnation required that Christ's humanity should be that of a particular man—a Palestinian Jew of the first century. In order to show forth the full scope of Christ's redeeming intention, it was therefore necessary that what was lacking in His individual existence should be "filled up" for His Body, the Church (cf. Col 1:24). The missionary expansiveness of the Church is requisite for the manifestation of this salvific universalism. If Christianity were content to flourish only in a single nation or continent, or a single ethnic or cultural group, the Church would not sufficiently exhibit its true nature as a universal sacrament of salvation. It would lack what we may call "semeiological catholicity," i.e., universality in its capacity as sign.

On this view it immediately becomes apparent that the missions are not a work of supererogation performed with lordly munificence. The Church does not distribute the alms of the gospel from its swelling purse simply to alleviate the spiritual penury of others. On the contrary, the missions correspond to a true inner exigency of the Church. Just as every individual person is driven by an ineradicable instinct to express his personality, and achieves adulthood through such authentic self-expression, so the Church achieves its maturity through showing forth, in concrete historical visibility, its universal mission as instrument of divine salvation.

But still we must explain how this semeiological catholicity, as I have called it, contributes to the salvation of the nations to whom the Church is sent. Here we encounter a deep mystery similar to that which lies at the root of all sacramental causality. I doubt that we can get an adequate explanation in terms of the classical theories of causality, such as those of Aristotle. Some modern theologians, who appear to be on the right track, maintain that the problem is insoluble unless we overcome the atomistic and somewhat mechanical individualism of modern Western thought-patterns and return to the rich biblical concepts of corporate personality and collective responsibility. In particular, the biblical idea of representation or deputyship is here of prime importance. Just as the first Adam represented and brought about the sinfulness of our fallen race, so Christ, the second Adam, redeemed mankind by way of representation. In line with this approach, we can say that the Church, under Christ, must effect the application of Christ's redemptive power by representing mankind in its redeemed existence. To become such a sign, the Church must constantly strive to make itself genuinely representative of mankind in all the diversity of its ethnic and cultural strains. Only by incarnating the Word of God, as far as possible, among all peoples can the full import of Christ's salvific work be properly signified.

The effectiveness of this redemptive power for the salvation of individuals depends, of course, on their personal dispositions. If they effectively lean forward to the "good news" before it is actually preached to them, their intention in some way meets the active missionary intention of the Church itself in a way that brings about salvation. It is not necessary that each individual should actually hear and accept the gospel, provided he really tends toward it. The acceptance of the gospel, however, will alone bring fulfilment to the aspirations obscurely at work in his soul.

Fr. Eugene Hillman, in his exciting little book *The Church as Mission*,[3] develops ideas basically consonant with what we have just been saying. But he adds a further refinement of his own, namely, that the establishment of the Church in any particular region is an efficacious sign of the redemption of the particular ethnic-cultural group among whom the Church now comes into being. Since past, present, and future are all the same in God's eyes, he adds, this efficacy can extend backward and forward in time, and thus include the ancestors and descendants of the people presently evangelized. From this he concludes that it is necessary for the completion of salvation history that the gospel should have been preached among each people at some time before the end of the world, and he implies that once this evangelization has occurred it is relatively unimportant whether a people perseveres in the faith. He thus paints a picture of a Church which travels from place to

[3] New York: Herder and Herder, 1965.

place like a summer-stock company until the evangelization of all the nations has been accomplished.

I personally find it hard to accept the theological significance which Hillman gives to the ethnic-cultural divisions of the human race. His view seems to give no explanation of how there can be any possibility of salvation for members of a tribe or nation that became extinct before the time of Christ or the arrival of Christian missionaries. Furthermore, Hillman seems to make too little of the concern which the Church has always felt to expand its membership within each people, and to insist upon their perseverance in the faith which they have once accepted.

Hillman's book brings out very well the idea that the primary task of the mission is not to convert every individual but rather to raise up a visible sign of the universality of Christian redemption. This thesis, which I regard as unassailable, involves important consequences for the conduct of the missions. On the negative side, it should liberate missionaries from any excessive preoccupation with statistics. The number of conversions and baptisms, while it may be significant, does not tell the whole story. What is of chief importance is that the reality of the Church be incarnated in each people to whom the gospel is preached. The missionary would not have achieved his task if he converted the entire population of a given area, unless he also succeeded in implanting the Church there as an autochthonous reality. As long as the Church exists under alien forms, and presents the aspect of a foreign enclave, the mission has not achieved itself; for catholicity, as I have already said, is a qualitative rather than a sheerly quantitative term.

This gives rise to some reflections on the idea of accommodation, which has always been a key concept in missiology. If catholicity is quantitatively regarded, the aim of the mission will be to insert as many individuals as possible into a Church which is conceived as being fully constituted with all its organs and habitual forms of action. On such a theory, accommodation becomes a mere expedient for winning converts. The gospel is presented in a form which makes it as easy as possible for the natives to accept. So conceived, accommodation is always tinged with a patronizing attitude, and a dangerous pragmatism is introduced into the work of evangelization.

According to the documents of Vatican II, accommodation has positive theological significance. "This accommodated preaching of the revealed word ought to remain the law of all evangelization," says the Constitution on the Church in the Modern World (n. 44). In accordance with the principle of incarnation, it is mandatory that the gospel be introduced as an indigenous element in every ethnic and cultural situation where it is preached. "For thus each nation develops the ability to express Christ's message in its own way. At the same time, a living exchange is fostered between the Church and the diverse cultures of people" (*ibid.*). To treat Christianity as an abstract essence, which must be realized in identical forms in every land, is to violate the demand that the Word be made flesh.

An interesting example of how the catechumenate might be adapted to certain missionary situations is proposed in the Constitution on the Liturgy. Since many tribes have initiation rites, elements from these, it is suggested, might be included, with necessary adaptations, in the liturgy of the catechumenate (nn. 64–65). It is, of course, understood that the Church cannot take over anything from the pagan cultures without purifying it and elevating it to make it truly Christian. Accommodation does not authorize the retention of pagan superstitions of the African and Asiatic peoples any more than those of the Irish and Italians.

In connection with the question of accommodation, it is well to keep in mind that the missions aim to enrich not only the peoples being evangelized but also the Church itself. Insofar as the Christian faith is incarnated in the various cultures of the world, each people is able to bring its particular gift to the universal Church. As stated in article 13 of *Lumen gentium:* "In virtue of this catholicity each individual part of the Church contributes through its special gifts to the good of the other parts and of the whole Church." The same thought recurs in the Decree on Ecumenism, which notes that the divisions among Christians prevent the Church from achieving and expressing its full catholicity in all its aspects (n. 4j). For Catholic unity, as has often been observed, does not mean uniformity. As a polyphonic harmony, it is actually promoted by the preservation of legitimate differences among various peoples. In the words of *Lumen gentium:* "The variety of local churches with one common aspiration is particularly splendid evidence of the catholicity of the undivided Church" (n. 23f).

In the full perspectives of Vatican II, missionary activity appears no longer as a simple imposition of the truth of the gospel upon a human culture which was indifferent towards it. Rather it is seen to be the joint fulfilment of the Church's inner drive to express its catholicity and of the secret aspirations of the nations to make conscious contact with their divine Redeemer. Contemporary Catholic teaching is beginning to spell out the implications of the ancient doctrine that God bestows His grace outside the visible limits of the Church and that all grace tends toward the Church as the locus of its fulfilment. The theory of "anonymous Christianity," to which I have already referred, makes it necessary to recognize that the grace of God runs ahead of the preachers of the gospel, preparing the way for them. Christianity does not have to be injected into men's lives from outside, like an alien substance; it really is, and should be credibly presented as, an answer to their needs, anxieties, and God-given aspirations. By failing to adapt the forms of Christianity to the circumstances of various peoples, the missionary effort has often fallen short of its true potential. An unhealthy division has often been set up in the spiritual lives of the new Christians, who must receive and practice their Christianity in foreign dress.

Accommodation may be regarded as a two-way street. If the manner in which the gospel is proposed must be adapted to the conditions of particular audiences, the audiences must also adjust their own ideas and customs to the Christian message. In order to appreciate the good news of what God has done for man, they must be familiarized through education with the main lines of salvation history and with the riches of the Bible. Dom Bernard Botte, O.S.B., has quite rightly protested against the hasty action of a zealous priest who eliminated the names of Abel, Abraham, and Melchizedek from his translation of the Canon of the Mass on the ground that the people had no idea who these persons were.[4]

[4] "The Problem of Adaptation in the Liturgy," in Robert E. Campbell, M.M. (ed.), *The Church in Mission* (Maryknoll, N.Y.: Maryknoll Publications, 1965) pp. 143–44.

A proper spirit of accommodation must restrain missionaries from crudely Westernizing peoples who legitimately fear the loss of what is precious and distinctive in their own heritage. On the other hand, the missionary must beware of a false primitivism which would link the Church too closely to tribal customs which are being outgrown. Rather he must prudently help the indigenous peoples in their efforts to rise to a higher level of culture and technology.

The promotion of authentic human values should not be regarded opportunistically as a mere device for building up contacts and relationships which may eventually result in conversions to the faith. A more comprehensive view of the mission of the Church should make it evident that missionaries are fulfilling their task whenever they promote those values which help to create that universal brotherhood of love to which God calls all men in Christ. The missions are the outstretched hand of the Church seeking to extend and deepen that brotherhood. A society in which men are bound together in true civic friendship may be regarded as an adumbration, as yet perhaps anonymous, of the proper reality of the Church. The Church in its full institutional reality should be a symbol and expression of this divinely given charity.

The making of converts will always have a place in missionary work. But the term itself is too crude to express the variety of goals which should be kept in view in accordance with the ecclesiology of Vatican II. It is no longer sufficient to divide the human race into two great classes, members and nonmembers of the Church. In its second chapter *Lumen gentium* shows that individuals or groups may be related to the Church by a plurality of bonds, some of which can exist in the absence of others. Every positive link with Christ and His Church is to be fostered and cherished, even when it does not amount to formal membership. For the missionary, this means that he will be achieving part of this task whenever he is able to sustain, purify, or perfect anything humanly valid in the cultures of the peoples to whom he is sent.

The brevity of this survey prohibits us from discussing at appropriate length the "loving and sincere dialogue" which Vatican II has sought to foster between Christianity and the other religions. That dialogue is not alien to the missionary effort, but intimately connected with it. It enables the Christian and non-Christian to speak and listen to one another with openness and love. A dialogue of this kind, while it may not lead to conversions, is justified on other grounds. The missionary attains part of his goal if he makes it possible for the Church to assimilate something of the spiritual experience of the peoples who have not yet accepted Christianity, and if he can communicate certain Christian values and attitudes to them. The resulting bonds between Christian and non-Christian may be reckoned among those salvific links by which the mystery of Christ and the Church becomes a leaven throughout the world.

If direct evangelization is more difficult in our day than at some times in the past, we have the consolation that ours is an age generally favorable to fruitful religious dialogue. The signs of the times would seem to require that all the major world religions take cognizance of this situation. The increasingly close social, technical, and cultural bonds, linking the entire human race into a common spiritual history, lend special emphasis to the Church's missionary task, as indicated in article 1 of *Lumen gentium*.[5]

The preceding pages have concentrated on the missionary implications of the first two chapters of *Lumen gentium*, and this is where I should like the emphasis to rest. But anyone reading the remainder of the document will find other points of immense significance for missionary theory and practice. The third chapter, for instance, sets forth the principle of collegiality, clarifying the relations between the pope and the other bishops. Vatican I had emphasized the monarchic principle. Some concluded that individual bishops were responsible only for their own dioceses, and that foreign missions were the exclusive responsibility of the pope. The Code of Canon Law (canon 1350, par. 2) expressly declares that in territories where there is no local ordinary, the entire care of the missions is reserved to the Holy See alone. But Pius XII, in his missionary encyclicals, modified this view. Anticipating the recent Council, he declared in *Fidei donum* (1957): "If every bishop is the proper pastor of the flock entrusted to his care, his quality as a legitimate successor of the apostles by divine institution renders him jointly responsible for the apostolic mission of the Church" (n. 59). The Constitution *Lumen gentium*, in a passage dealing with the solicitude of each and every bishop for the welfare of the whole Church, makes specific mention of the missions: "It is the duty of all bishops . . . to foster every activity which is common to the whole Church, especially efforts to spread the faith and make the light of full truth dawn on all men" (n. 23c). In the following article the Constitution declares:

[5] Quoted above, p. 21.

"As successors of the apostles, bishops receive from Him [Christ] the mission to teach all nations and to preach the gospel to every creature, so that all men may attain to salvation by faith, baptism, and the fulfilment of the commandments." The consequences of this collective responsibility of all the bishops for the Church's total task of evangelization are spelled out in somewhat fuller detail in the Decree *Ad gentes*. In the future we may presumably expect that the territorial conferences of bishops, as well as the universal synod of bishops in Rome, will assume a larger responsibility for certain aspects of the missionary apostolate.

After treating of the bishops, *Lumen gentium* goes on to discuss the priests, as collaborators of the bishops and sharers in their concern for the universal Church. The principle of collegiality in a wide sense extends indirectly to priests as associates of the bishops. The presence of priests in mission areas has a special importance; for, as the Constitution explains in another context, although all the faithful can baptize, the priest alone can complete the building up of the Body of Christ in the Eucharistic sacrifice, thus fulfilling the oracle of Malachi in the Old Testament: "From the rising of the sun to its going down, my name is great among the Gentiles, and in every place there is sacrifice . . ." (n. 17c). Without the food of the Eucharist the Church can scarcely grow.

The provisions of chapter 3 concerning the restored diaconate are, of course, full of significance for mission lands, not only because deacons might be ordained locally, but also because deacons from areas where there are sufficient priests could perhaps be sent out as missionaries. The possible functions of permanent deacons in missionary regions are elaborated with further particulars in *Ad gentes*, n. 16.

Chapter 4 of *Lumen gentium*, concerning the laity, states very concisely the main principles concerning the missionary role of lay people, and thus lays the groundwork for the more detailed statements found in the Decrees on Missionary Activity and on the Lay Apostolate. *Lumen gentium* makes it clear that the lay apostolate is not a rare vocation but an inalienable responsibility laid upon each of the faithful through baptism and confirmation. Every layman is called upon to be a witness of the gospel in his personal life; as a member of the Church, he should seek to contribute to its missionary apostolate by his own understanding, enthusiasm, talents, prayers, and material resources. Some laymen will be called by divine grace to go abroad as lay missionaries, either permanently or for a period of time. Others, who travel to mission lands for reasons of business or pleasure, can wonderfully assist in the apostolate of the Church by the example of their personal and professional lives, as well as by their active participation in Church functions. The charitable and social work which forms an indispensable part of the missionary endeavor can profit enormously from the assistance of competent laymen.

The following two chapters of *Lumen gentium*, on the universal call to holiness and on the religious, have important implications for missionary spirituality. It has always been recognized that the missionary must be eminent in his ability to forsake the ordinary comforts of life and conspicuous in his zeal for the kingdom of Christ. This is true on any theory of the missions. But the theory we have followed in this chapter, namely, that the mission must be first of all a sign of the presence of God's universal redemptive love, makes it all-important that the missionary himself should be a man of Christlike charity. The manner in which evangelization is done is even more important than its apparent success. The basic principle is splendidly expressed in *Lumen gentium*, n. 8:

Just as Christ carried out the work of redemption in poverty and under oppression, so the Church is called to follow the same path in communicating to men the fruits of salvation. Christ Jesus, "though He was by nature God, . . . emptied Himself, taking on the nature of a slave" (Phil 2:6), and "being rich, He became poor" (2 Cor 8:9) for our sakes. Thus, although the Church needs human resources to carry out her mission, she is not set up to seek earthly glory, but to proclaim humility and self-sacrifice, even by her own example.

The Church in mission areas, while it may properly seek to disseminate the benefits of modern science and technology, must not appear as an island of affluence in a sea of poverty and squalor. Rather it must be content to walk the path of poverty, self-abnegation, and obedience, and deliberately identify itself with the poor and needy of the region where it finds itself. The patience of a Charles de Foucauld and the sufferings of an Isaac Jogues, because they dramatically mirror the selfless charity of Christ Himself, are better signs of the Church's dynamic catholicity than the visible successes of many skilled convert makers.

In this connection some mention should be made of the principles regarding proselytization set forth in the Declaration on Religious Liberty. Insisting on the freedom of the act of faith, the Church here condemns "any manner of action which might seem to carry a hint of coercion or a kind of persuasion that would be dishonorable or unworthy, especially in dealing with poor or uneducated people" (n. 4). To some this renunciation might appear as an onerous restriction on missionary zeal. But if missionary activity is viewed as Christian witness, it is quite evident that the truth of the gospel cannot be imposed by force or threats. "Rather it is established and it extends its dominion by the love whereby Christ, lifted up on the cross, draws all men to Himself" (n. 11).

Returning to *Lumen gentium*, chapter 6, we should not overlook the strong praise given to the religious orders for their contribution to the missions. This is something more than a polite acknowledgment of services rendered in the past. It is a recognition that the witness of the religious life has a special power of its own, as a sign of the gospel and of the triumphant "eschatological" grace of Christ. The total renunciation implied in the vows shows forth, much as martyrdom does, the incomparable riches of the love of God. By virtue of the state they have entered, the religious in mission lands are obliged to manifest by their devotion to prayer and works of charity, by their humility and self-denial, the totality of their dedication to Christ and to the whole human family.

The last two chapters of *Lumen gentium* are of great importance for missionary theology, because they place the Church's apostolate within the framework of Christian eschatology. They clearly point out that the Church's task will never be achieved within historical time, but only by the decisive intervention through which Christ will establish His final kingdom. But before this harvest can occur, when the Church will be gathered from the four winds, the gospel must first be preached to all the nations (Mk 13:10; cf. Decree on Missionary Activity, n. 9). When the Lord returns, and only then, will the gap between the sign of the Church and the reality of God's redemptive work be removed. In the heavenly liturgy, as we read in *Lumen gentium*, "all those from every tribe and tongue and people and nation (cf. Ap 5:9) who have been redeemed by the blood of Christ and gathered together into one Church, with one song of praise magnify the triune God" (n. 50). In all its missionary activity the Church must be sustained by the confident hope of that final day when, as the last paragraph of the Constitution on the Church reminds us, "all the peoples of the human family, whether they are honored with the name of Christian or whether they still do not know their Saviour, [will be] happily gathered together in peace and harmony into the one People of God, to the glory of the most holy and undivided Trinity."

⋆ 4 ⋆

The Church and the World

In the previous two chapters we have touched on two major areas of the Church's relations *ad extra:* relations with the other Christians and with those who are not Christians. In each case we have found that the Church is in a dialogue situation, in which it both gives and receives. We turn now to a third major area, the relations between the Church and the world. The world, as we here understand the term, is not an additional class of persons but the sum total of all those realities which pertain to man in his life here below and which confront him whether he is a believer or not. Within the life of one and the same man, if he is a Christian, the Church and the world are simultaneously present. The polarity of these relations gives rise to many practical tensions and theoretical dilemmas which are much debated in our day. How can we define the respective claims and spheres of the Church and the world?

The past few years have witnessed the production of an enormous quantity of literature on this thorny question. Protestants and Anglicans have written best sellers bearing titles such as *The Secular Meaning of the Gospel* (P. van Buren), *The Secularisation of Christianity* (E. L. Mascall), and *The Secular City* (H. Cox). Some non-Catholics press for an extreme reductionist solution which would say in effect that the Church must be judged only in terms of what it can contribute to the building of the city of man. Cox seems to imply this when he writes: "The Church is the sign of the emergent city of man, an outrider for the secular city." [1]

On the Catholic side, serious concern with the same problem is indicated by several recent collections of articles such as *The Christian and the World* [2] and *The Church and the World*. [3] Most of the essays in these two volumes favor nuanced solutions, accepting moderate forms of secularization but not to the exclusion of the sacred. The same tendency is reflected in the most original and characteristic document of Vatican II, the Pastoral Constitution on the Church in the Modern World, which we shall use as a principal source for the present chapter.

The problem of the world and its value in the sight of God has deep biblical roots. The Old Testament begins with the bold affirmation that God created the world and that it was good. But this affirmation can hardly be exploited as a proclamation of secularism. It occurs in the "priestly" creation account, a story cast in the pattern of seven days, ending with a Sabbath on which God Himself piously rests. The Old Testament firmly asserts that God's lordship extends not simply to a narrow sphere of religious events but to the whole government of nature and history, and it is with worldly affairs that the religious leaders and prophets of Israel are chiefly concerned. But in the later Old Testament books the two spheres tend to become more clearly distinct, as religious devotion becomes cen-

[1] Harvey Cox, *The Secular City* (New York: Macmillan, 1965) p. 145.
[2] New York: Kenedy, 1965.
[3] *Concilium* 6 (Glen Rock, N.J.: Paulist Press, 1965).

tered about the Torah and the Temple, and religious hope focuses on an apocalyptic action by which God will bring history as we know it to a close.

The New Testament, especially in the Johannine literature, exhibits an ambivalent attitude toward the world. Although God so loved the world as not to spare His own Son for its redemption, Christ, when He came, refused to pray for the world; He struggled unceasingly against the Prince of this world. In questions of morality and worship, Christ appears almost as a secularist. Proclaiming the hour when men everywhere would be able to worship in the spirit and in truth, He predicted the destruction of the Temple and supplanted the ceremonies and priesthood of the Old Law. The heart of religion, for Jesus, consisted in a love of God and neighbor which could be exercised in worldly situations. But He also referred to Himself as the new Temple. Wholly preoccupied with His Father's business, He refused to involve Himself in political and economic questions. He chose disciples, trained them for specifically religious tasks, and empowered them to preach the word and to perform sacred rites in His name.

Distinctions between the sacred and the secular, the city of God and the city of man, the things of God and the things of Caesar, the Church and the world became characteristic of Christianity almost from the beginning. The Middle Ages witnessed a luxuriant growth of the sacred as sign and symbol of God's presence in the visible world. Medieval thinking was markedly hierarchical. It looked upon the sacred as superior to the secular in view of its greater proximity to the divine. At least in theory, the Church, as a sacred society, had the last word on practically every question. It kept a watchful eye over the arts and sciences, affairs of state, even wars and commerce. The sacred ministrations of religion were considered essential for obtaining health of body, success in military operations, good harvests, etc. Revealed religion was supposed to offer the surest guide for philosophy and to secure the very foundations of science. Theology, as queen, looked upon the other sciences as her handmaids.

The rediscovery of Aristotle marks an initial stage in the decline of sacral civilization. Thomism made an effort to give the new logic and philosophy their due, and yet keep them under the hegemony of theology. In the Renaissance, however, the arts and sciences declared themselves fully independent of religious controls, while at the same time the political powers of the West cast off their allegiance to pope and emperor. In this respect humanism, the scientific revolution, and the growth of national sovereignty are all related phenomena.

The Protestant Reformation was not unconnected with this trend toward secularity. Luther first sounded the battle cry against holy places, holy things, and holy persons. His personal transition from the monastic to the married state is symbolic of the general movement of sixteenth-century Protestantism. Luther's views concerning the Sacrifice of the Mass, indulgences, the invocation of saints, and the ecclesiastical hierarchy may all be interpreted as reactions against the exorbitant sacramentalism of the Late Middle Ages. Within the Christian community, Luther attached little importance to hierarchical stratifications:

Everyone who has been baptized may claim that he has already been consecrated priest, bishop, or pope, even though it is not seemly for any particular person arbitrarily to exercise the office.

. . . Hence we deduce that there is, at bottom, really no other difference between laymen, priests, princes, bishops, or in Romanist terminology, between religious and secular, than that of office or occupation, and not that of Christian status.[4]

While one cannot identify Protestantism unequivocally with secular Christianity, it seems correct to say that Protestant morality has on the whole been more worldly and less sacral than Catholic morality. In Puritanism, for example, the "hard work" of the citizen did duty for the "good works" of the medieval monk. The religious conscience of the Puritan was harnassed to the virtues of thrift, industry, and civic responsibility rather than to exercises of piety, although the latter were by no means neglected.

In our own day the secular tide has risen to a new high. More and more functions which used to be considered properly religious are taken over by government agencies or by private organizations without any definite religious affiliation. Although the churches continue to run hospitals, schools, and charitable societies of their own, they are faced with more and stiffer secular competition in these fields. Some feel that the sacred dimension of life is receding to the point of eventual nonexistence.

Three characteristic reactions to the phenomenon of secularization are in evidence. First, there are the unbelieving secularists, who hold that the trend is irreversible and portends the end of the Christian era. Reason and science, they hold, rather than sacred doctrine and churchly ministrations, must be used for the solution of all human problems.

Secondly, there is the reaction of the conservative

4 "An Appeal to the Ruling Class," in J. Dillenberger, *Martin Luther: Selections* (Garden City, New York: Anchor Books, 1961) p. 409.

Christian, who, identifying Christianity closely with the sacred, deplores the progress of secularization as a great defection, perhaps even as a sign of the approach of Antichrist.

Thirdly, there is the view of contemporary radical Christianity, which welcomes secularization and maintains that it is fully compatible with the true Christian message, duly demythologized. Does not the Bible teach that God made the world good and commanded man to exercise dominion over it? In our final chapter we shall examine Dietrich Bonhoeffer, one of the most influential spokesmen of secular Christianity.

To understand this third position, it is important to see why the category of the sacred is widely questioned and even rejected in our time. The concept itself is a very difficult one. The "sacred" normally denotes some temporal reality specially appropriated to God: e.g., a time of year (a holy day or season), a place (sacred grove, shrine, etc.), an object (book, chalice, or the like), an action (e.g., a vow, a ritual), a person (one consecrated by vows or holy orders). For anything to become sacred, there is need of some special type of event attributed to God (e.g., a miracle, an extraordinary grace, a sacrament). The sacred reality is thereafter looked upon as a sign which expresses and calls to mind what God has done.

For contemporary man, all this smacks of mythological thinking. Tending to look upon history as a seamless web, he wants to explain events in this world by inner-worldly causes; he is suspicious about events attributed to the direct action of God. Supposedly sacred objects make him uneasy. Far from arousing in him a sense of the numinous, they often impress him as unauthentic, even faintly ridiculous. He is on guard against being taken in by superstition and pious mumbo jumbo. Even when he does feel moved to awe and wonder, he is not inclined to set a very high value on these sentiments. He suspects that a life too sharply concentrated on the divine or the otherworldly would be an immoral delusion; it would distract him from his duties in the earthly city. The heroism of a life "thrown away" upon God looks too much like an evasion of responsibility. The image of the stylite or the anchorite has lost its appeal. An authentically Christian life, in the eyes of most men today, must be able to exhibit good fruits in terms of helping other men. "By their fruits you shall know them." Thus a certain Christian secularity has an undoubted appeal for the contemporary Western mind.

Vatican Council II took cognizance of the urgent problems posed by Christian secularity. This was an issue which the Council simply could not dodge. In the following pages we shall attempt to recapitulate the main conclusions set forth in the conciliar documents, especially in the Pastoral Constitution *Gaudium et spes*.[5] Our first task will be to clarify the meaning of the terms "world" and "Church."

The notion of the "world" is most fully explained in the opening paragraphs of *Gaudium et spes*. In article 2 it is described as "the whole human family along with the sum of those realities in the midst of which the human family lives." This world, we are then told, is "the theater of man's history, and carries with it the marks of his energies,

[5] In the rest of this chapter the Latin titles used for documents of Vatican II correspond to the following English titles: *Apostolicam actuositatem* = Decree on the Apostolate of the Laity; *Dei verbum* = Dogmatic Constitution on Divine Revelation; *Gaudium et spes* = Pastoral Constitution on the Church in the Modern World; *Lumen gentium* = Dogmatic Constitution on the Church; *Sacrosanctum concilium* = Constitution on the Liturgy; *Unitatis redintegratio* = Decree on Ecumenism.

his tragedies, and his triumphs." Fallen into the bondage of sin, this world is nevertheless emancipated in principle by Christ, who was crucified in order to break the stranglehold of evil, "so that this world might be fashioned anew according to God's design and reach its fulfilment." Since the world is involved in sin, man must approach it with caution. In another context, therefore, the Council repeats the Apostle's warning, "Be not conformed to this world" (Rom 12:2), and immediately adds that the world in this context means "that spirit of vanity and malice which transforms into an instrument of sin those human energies intended for the service of God and man" (*Gaudium et spes*, n. 37). While the world is evil by reason of sin, it is also capable of redemption, and has in greater or lesser degree already been restored by Christ.

As appears from the previous chapters of this study, the term "Church" may be understood either as organization or as community. In the former sense, it is an institution distinct from other "worldly" institutions; it is a sacramental sign and agent of that saving unity of mankind which God intends to establish in Christ. In the second aspect, the Church is that portion of mankind which is visibly gathered into the Body of Christ and which lives by His Spirit. It stands where God wills the whole world to stand. The Church as institution prays and labors "that the entire world may become the People of God, the Body of the Lord, and the Temple of the Holy Spirit" (*Lumen gentium*, n. 17).

The Church exists, no doubt, in order to serve the world, but the service which it is required and equipped to render is a very special one. "The Church has a single intention: that God's kingdom may come, and that the sal-

[73]

vation of the whole human race may come to pass" (*Gaudium et spes*, n. 45). Thus, before we can clarify the relation of the Church to the world, we must explain the notion of God's kingdom. Is it something to be realized in this world or in another? Is it achieved by man's labor or by God's intervention?

In its finished form, it may be described as that "kingdom of truth and life, of holiness and grace, of justice, love, and peace" which Christ will hand over to His Father at the end of time (*ibid.*, n. 39). But it is already inchoatively present on earth. According to *Lumen gentium*, the central message of Christ's public ministry was that "the time is fulfilled, and the kingdom of God is at hand." The arrival of the kingdom was revealed in Jesus' words, in His miraculous deeds, and most of all in His very person. When He came to the end of His earthly career, He commanded and equipped His Church to continue His mission of proclaiming and establishing the kingdom of God (n. 5). The kingdom is now present in mystery; it will display itself with full clarity in heaven (*Gaudium et spes*, n. 39).

How is the advent and growth of the kingdom related to man's earthly progress? On this most pressing question of our day, the Council gave a few general but very helpful indications. Negatively, it declared that the establishment of God's kingdom is not identical with man's earthly progress (*ibid.*); it comes about not through the immanent development of worldly energies but through the descending action of God. Since God Himself freely establishes the kingdom by His gracious intervention, it cannot be a simple result of human industry. The final stage of the kingdom will be in some measure discontinuous with the history that leads up to it; it will fulfil earthly values, but in a transcendent manner, "freed from stain, burnished, and transfigured" (*ibid.*). Entrance into the kingdom of God, therefore, involves a passage through a kind of death. It is not a simple expansion or evolution from a prior state, but a radically new state of being.

On the other hand, there is a positive relationship between earthly realities and the kingdom of God. The new heavens and the new earth will be fashioned out of those which we now know. "For here grows the body of the new human family, a body which even now is able to give some kind of foreshadowing of the new age" (*ibid.*). By cultivating the earth we prepare the material of the celestial realm (*ibid.*, n. 38). While the Council does not say that such human activity is a necessary condition for the advent of the Parousia, its teaching blends admirably with the affirmative view of many modern theologians. Teilhard de Chardin, as is well known, believed that the final Parousia, while resulting from the transcendent action of God, was nonetheless conditioned by the activity of man, who must through love build the earthly city in its highest form.[6] Karl Rahner speaks in somewhat similar terms when he declares: "The consummation to be brought about by God does not, in the last analysis, expect a dead but a living humanity which has gone to its very limits and so is burst open by salvation from above by developing its own powers." [7]

Vatican II, therefore, points toward a middle path between a supernaturalism which would press the initiative of God at the expense of the proper activity of man, and a naturalism which would look upon the kingdom of heaven

[6] Cf. C. F. Mooney, S.J., *Teilhard de Chardin and the Mystery of Christ* (New York: Harper & Row, 1966) pp. 181–88.

[7] "Christianity and the 'New Man,'" in *The Christian and the World* (cited n. 2 above) p. 224.

as a merely human achievement. This balanced position, which we have observed in the eschatological teaching of the Council, is likewise evident in its Christology, its ecclesiology, and in its doctrine concerning the states in life. We shall briefly touch upon each of these areas.

Whereas Church teaching in recent centuries has concentrated almost exclusively on Christ as Redeemer—that is, as saving man from a sinful world—the present Council goes back to the teaching of Paul, John, and the early Fathers in portraying Christ as Lord of all things. Just as one and the same God is "Saviour and Creator, Lord of human history as well as of salvation history" (*Gaudium et spes*, n. 41), so Christ is the crown of the order of creation as well as that of redemption. As Alpha and Omega, He is the source and final goal of both orders (*ibid.*, n. 45):

For God's Word, by whom all things were made, was Himself made flesh so that as perfect man He might save all men and sum up all things in Himself. The Lord is the goal of human history, the focal point of the longings of history and of civilization, the center of the human race, the joy of every heart, and the answer to all its yearnings. . . . Enlivened and united in His Spirit, we journey toward the consummation of human history, one which fully accords with the counsel of God's love: "to re-establish all things in Christ, both those in the heavens and those on the earth" (Eph 1:10).

The mission of the Church, as described in Vatican II, does not have the same all-embracing universality as that of Christ. In contrast with some extreme representatives of Christian secularity, the Council teaches that the Church's primary and direct mission is not temporal but spiritual. "Christ . . . gave His Church no proper mission in the political, economic, or social order. The purpose which He set before her is a religious one" (*ibid.*, n. 42). Reminding men that "the structure of this world is passing away," the Church must continually caution them not to get "bogged down" in this world (*ibid.*).

In chapter 1 we have spoken of the teaching of *Lumen gentium* on the eschatological orientation of the Church. The same emphasis is evident in the Constitution on the Liturgy, which because of its subject matter naturally gives special prominence to the sacred. Liturgical worship is extolled as "the summit toward which the activity of the Church is directed" and "the fountain from which all her power flows" (n. 10). The liturgy, we are told, is by no means subservient to the apostolate; rather the apostolate is ordered toward the goal that "all who are made sons of God by faith and baptism should come together to praise God in the midst of His Church, to take part in her sacrifice, and to eat the Lord's Supper." The pre-eminent value of the liturgy is justified by reference to the eschatological destiny of the Church. "In the earthly liturgy, by way of foretaste, we share in that heavenly liturgy which is celebrated in the holy city of Jerusalem toward which we journey as pilgrims" (n. 8). These strong affirmations in the Council's first major document cannot be simply ignored by anyone who wishes to assimilate the mind of Vatican II. While later Council documents show a greater concern with the temporal order, they do not cancel out the teaching in the Constitution on the Liturgy.

In its later documents the Council has much to say to those Christians of our time who feel distressed by the apparent irrelevance of religion to the goals of man's temporal life. In general, the Church may be said to serve "as a leaven or as a kind of soul for human society as it is to be renewed in Christ and transformed into God's family" (*Gaudium et spes*, n. 40). The idea of "soul" recalls the famous statement in the *Letter to Diognetus* cited in *Lumen gentium* (n. 38): "What the soul is to the body, let Christians be to the world."

The various benefits which the Church brings to the world, as enumerated by the Council, may perhaps be grouped under three headings. In the first place, the Church recognizes the intrinsic goodness of the natural order and the dignity of man as a created person. It therefore respects the just autonomy of the arts and sciences, and defends their integrity against intrusion (*Gaudium et spes*, nn. 36, 59). Secondly, it has a healing office, insofar as it applies the medicine of grace to repair the ravages wrought by sin (*ibid.*, n. 37). Since Christ Himself was perfect man, those who follow Him are restored to the fulness of their humanity (*ibid.*, n. 40). Finally, the Church has an elevating influence insofar as it draws man into union with God and thus gives human dignity its fullest expansion (*ibid.*, n. 21). The whole temporal order, by reason of its essential relatedness to man, participates in his call to eternal blessedness (*Apostolicam actuositatem*, n. 7). Paul, in the eighth chapter of Romans, poetically depicts the whole world as longing to share in the glorification of the sons of God at the end of time.

This multiform beneficent influence the Church exercises through its three functions of witness, ministry, and fellowship. When the Church as God's witness proclaims the saving tidings of salvation, it answers to the deepest aspirations of the human heart and brings light, life, and freedom to those who accept its word in faith (*Gaudium et spes*, n. 21). The doctrinal office of the Church serves to illumine the meaning of man's temporal life (*Lumen gentium*, n. 48) and thus paves the way for a keener and more intelligent participation in human affairs—a point which the Decree on Education develops in its explanation of the Church's role as educator.

Secondly, the Church through its activity seeks always to relieve human want and distress and to mirror the features of Christ the Servant (*Unitatis redintegratio*, n. 12). It urges its sons to join eagerly in the task of building up the city of man. This duty, as we have noted, rests upon man in view of the biblical doctrine that he received from the moment of creation the commission to subdue the earth. The Christian's confidence in the ultimate coming of God's kingdom, far from prompting him to idleness, gives him additional motives for human service (*Gaudium et spes*, nn. 21, 39). By neglecting our earthly duties we risk exclusion from the kingdom of heaven (*ibid.*, n. 43), whereas by cultivating the earth we prepare the material for the heavenly city (*ibid.*, n. 38).

Finally, by its internal fellowship the Church provides a beacon which should be capable of inspiring men with hope and charity. The unity of the Church, binding together in a single community men of all races under heaven, redounds to the advantage of the human family (*ibid.*, n. 42). As we have previously noted, the Church is, "by her relationship with Christ, both a sacramental sign and an instrument of intimate union with God, and of the unity of all mankind" (*Lumen gentium*, n. 1).

It may, of course, be objected at this point that the Church has in actual fact failed to exert the various beneficent influences which we have been describing. Without wishing to blacken the record of history, which contains many bright passages, one may admit that the Church has fallen far below the ideal. The Council repeatedly stresses the need of renewal and reform so that the lovable features of Christ may be more clearly reflected in the life of the Church. The faith of Christians "needs to prove its fruitfulness by penetrating the believer's entire life, including its worldly dimensions, and by activating him toward justice and love, especially regarding the needy" (*Gaudium et spes*, n. 21). To the extent that believers "neglect their own training in the faith, or teach erroneous doctrine, or are deficient in their religious, moral or social life, they must be said to conceal rather than reveal the authentic face of God and religion" (*ibid.*, n. 19).

The twofold relationship of the Church to the kingdom of God and to the city of man gives Christians a dual citizenship, both heavenly and earthly (*ibid.*, n. 43). To some it will be given to show forth one aspect of this citizenship, to others another. The diversity of vocations and their fundamental unity of purpose are concisely explained in *Gaudium et spes* (n. 38):

> Now, the gifts of the Spirit are diverse. He calls some to give clear witness to the desire for a heavenly home and to keep that desire green among the human family. He summons others to dedicate themselves to the earthly service of man and to make ready the material of the celestial realm by this ministry of theirs. Yet He frees all of them so that by putting aside love of self and bringing all earthly resources into the service of human life they can devote themselves to that future when humanity itself will become an offering accepted by God.

As Hans Urs von Balthasar has maintained,[8] the contrast between the lay and religious states in the Church is grounded in the twofold role of Christ as Son of Man and Son of God. Just as He fulfilled the dynamisms at work in the religious history of Israel and at the same time transcended them by a kind of dialectical negation, so the Christian life in its various forms must seek to express both the fulfilment of man's authentic aspirations and man's trustful self-surrender into the hands of a loving God. These ascending and descending aspects of ecclesial life are manifested respectively in the lay and religious states.

The special function of the laity, according to the Council documents, is to sanctify the world from within, in the manner of a leaven (*Lumen gentium*, n. 31). "The layman is closely involved in temporal affairs of every sort. It is therefore his special task to illumine and organize these affairs in such a way that they may always begin, develop, and persist according to the mind of Christ, to the praise of the Creator and Redeemer" (*ibid.*).

In one passage of the chapter on the laity (n. 34), *Lumen gentium* describes the function of sanctifying the world from within as a "consecration of the world." The phrase has been criticized and is perhaps ambiguous. In the ordinary meaning of the term, as Père Chenu points out, consecration involves a withdrawal of something from the world in order to devote it exclusively to God.[9] On this definition it would make no sense to say that the world itself is consecrated. But the term is here used in a wider

---

[8] *A Theology of History* (New York: Sheed & Ward, 1963) pp. 115–30.

[9] "*Consecratio mundi*," in *The Christian and the World*, p. 165.

sense to designate a transformation of the world into the kingdom of God. The Church's work in the temporal order, insofar as it tends to lead the world toward its eschatological consummation, cannot be adequately described in the vocabulary of the secular. Just as the eternal Word of God, by His presence among men, may be said to have consecrated the world,[10] so the Church, by sanctifying man's activity, gives the world a certain kind of sacredness.

The religious vocation, however, is more strictly related to the sacred. By its very nature it is a sign of the kingdom of God. Those who adopt a way of life according to the evangelical counsels, *Lumen gentium* declares, eloquently foretell the blessings of the resurrected state and show forth the powerful working of God's grace in this life (n. 44).

Like the religious, the clergy are primarily devoted to the sacred aspects of religion. They are "chiefly and professedly ordained to the sacred ministry" (*ibid.*, n. 31). Bishops, priests, and deacons, in their several degrees, are endowed with "sacred power" for the "nurturing and constant growth of the People of God" (*ibid.*, n. 18).

The conciliar documents, however, avoid too rigid a dichotomy between the vocations of laity and clergy, or secular and religious. The opposition is in some respects more one of degree and emphasis than strictly of kind. The dimension of the sacred is to be found in the life of every Christian. Thanks to the sacraments of baptism and confirmation, the laity themselves are consecrated to Christ, and have a consequent obligation "to spread and defend the faith both by word and deed as true witnesses of Christ"

[10] As we read in the Roman Martyrology for Christmas Day, "mundum volens adventu suo piissimo consecrare."

(*ibid.*, n. 11). When priests are lacking or are impeded, as in times of persecution, laymen may be called upon to perform many sacred ministries (*ibid.*, n. 35). Some lay persons, moreover, unselfishly "devote themselves entirely to apostolic work" without detriment to their lay status.

Conversely, priests and religious can perform certain temporal functions. "Those in holy orders can at times engage in secular activities, and even have a secular profession" (*ibid.*, n. 30). The consecration of religious does not make them "strangers to their fellow men or useless citizens of this earthly city," but gives spiritual support to those more directly engaged in temporal affairs, so that "the work of building up the earthly city can always have its foundation in the Lord and can tend toward Him" (*ibid.*, n. 46). Insofar as the religious life is a sign of the kingdom of God, it serves all Christians as a torch to direct their steps and to kindle their charity. "By their state in life, the religious give splendid and striking testimony that the world cannot be transfigured and offered to God without the spirit of the beatitudes" (*ibid.*, n. 31).

It is obvious that in our time many Christians fail to find in some of the outward forms of the liturgy and of the religious life a sign which effectively reminds them of Christ. The Council was conscious of this grave problem and sought to meet it by laying down prudent norms for renewal in both these areas. Bold experiments will probably be needed before the necessary progress can be made. In general, it may be said that we have here something similar to the problem discussed in the preceding chapter under the heading of missionary accommodation, for the missionary vocation of the Church extends not only to all geographical areas but to all chronological epochs.

After all we have said concerning the benefits which the Church renders to the world, it is necessary to add that the world affords great assistance to the Church. Vatican II goes far beyond all previous official statements of the Church in acknowledging this indebtedness. *Gaudium et spes* pays tribute to the progress of the arts and sciences for opening new roads to truths, clarifying the message of the gospel, and enabling it to be more effectively proclaimed (n. 44). The recent progress of biblical studies affords a striking instance of how sciences such as archeology can lead to a deeper understanding of the inspired text and in this way help to mature the judgment of the Church (cf. *Dei verbum*, n. 12). The conciliar Declaration on Religious Freedom pays tribute to modern developments in the political order for assisting the Church to develop its doctrine of religious liberty. Sociology, psychology, and the sciences of communication have far-reaching import for the renewal of the apostolate and of the spiritual life, as other Council documents acknowledge.

The ideal relationship between the Church and the world is, therefore, one of harmony within distinction. Until the ultimate transformation of all things, the world will retain a certain autonomy over against the Church. Created realities have a proper consistency of their own, and cannot be simply absorbed into the supernatural. We should not hope for the world to be transformed by some kind of cosmic transubstantiation into the Body of Christ. The Church and the world coexist in polar tension. Neither can get along without the other, but each retains its own nature and principles. The world will lose its way unless guided and sustained by the Church. But the Church will become ineffective unless it listens to the world. In our day, marked as it is by new and complex developments in many fields, it is particularly urgent for spokesmen of the Church to remain in close contact with specialists in the various arts and sciences (cf. *Gaudium et spes*, n. 44).

Such a two-way dialogue may appear scandalous to those who still think in terms of the medieval hierarchical scheme, according to which the Church is related to the world simply as ruler and teacher. But in point of fact this scheme never corresponded to the true situation. The actual realization of Christianity, as Karl Rahner observes, is always "the achieved synthesis on each occasion, of the message of the gospel and the grace of Christ, on the one hand, and of the concrete situation in which the gospel has to be lived, on the other." [11] For this reason Christianity, while it remains the same, is always different. To preach the gospel effectively, it is necessary to keep one ear open to the world. The Church cannot afford to ignore the world, any more than the world can afford to close its eyes to Christ and the Church.

The Church today, as it speaks to us through the documents of Vatican II, accepts many of the effects of modern secularization. Instead of hankering for a restoration of the medieval formula of unilateral subordination of the secular to the sacred, the Council unhesitatingly acknowledges that the secular disciplines have their inalienable autonomy and that human life can be sanctified without being removed from the world and transplanted into a special sphere of the sacred. But it is equally clear that the Council wishes to maintain the just prerogatives of the

[11] "Christianity and the 'New Man,'" p. 211.

sacred and not to dissolve the Church into a humanitarian social-service organization. Sacred doctrine, sacred rites, and a consecrated hierarchical priesthood, according to the institution of Christ, are essential features of Christianity. Without them the Church could not retain its full sacramental visibility or adequately sustain the eschatological hope of God's People throughout their earthly pilgrimage. Only in heaven, when God becomes all in all, will the tension between the secular and the sacred yield to perfect tranquility and to a joy that surpasses all understanding.

★ 5 ★

The Church in Bonhoeffer's "Worldly Christianity"

In chapter 4 we have already had occasion to mention Dietrich Bonhoeffer as one of the leading influences behind contemporary secular Christianity. Paul van Buren's *The Secular Meaning of the Gospel* begins with a long quotation from Bonhoeffer. J. A. T. Robinson and Harvey Cox show their indebtedness to him on nearly every page of their recent best sellers. William Hamilton, the controversial American death-of-God theologian, declares that his *New Essence of Christianity* is nothing more than an attempt to carry out Bonhoeffer's project of a work to be entitled *The Essence of Christianity*. "My essay as a whole," writes Hamilton, "is deeply indebted to Bonhoeffer, and may be taken as a theological response to the coming of age of the world as he has analyzed it." [1] Ved Mehta scarcely exaggerates when he writes: "The late Dietrich Bonhoeffer has probably affected more Christian theologians, and through them, more Christians of every sort than any other theologian of our time." [2]

Although the current Bonhoeffer cult may be something of a fad, there are solid reasons for including at this point a

[1] New York: Association Press, 1961, p. 12, n. 1.
[2] Ved Mehta, *The New Theologian* (New York: Harper & Row, 1966) pp. 13 f.

discussion of some aspects of his theology. A highly ecumenical thinker, he was conscious of the absurdity of the existing divisions between Protestant and Catholic Christianity. In spite of the iconoclastic ring of certain lapidary sentences which are constantly quoted—generally out of context—from his letters, he retained a deep loyalty to the ancient Christian heritage. And he succeeded in combining this loyalty with a truly prophetic sensitivity to the demands of the present age. Although he probably had little direct influence on the Council Fathers at Vatican II, his writings reflect many of the same concerns. Besides illuminating the phenomenon of Christian secularity, some treatment of Bonhoeffer should help to exhibit the possibilities and limits of the ecumenical theology of which we have spoken in chapter 2.

The broad outlines of Bonhoeffer's brief career have often been sketched. The son of a prominent neurologist and psychiatrist, he was raised in a highly cultured but rather agnostic household in Berlin. His two oldest brothers chose scientific careers, but Dietrich, while a student in high school (*Gymnasium*), decided on theology. After undergraduate studies at Tübingen, he received his licentiate in theology at Berlin in 1927. At that time he wrote a thesis on the theology of the Church under the liberal theologian Seeberg. Entitled *Sanctorum communio: A Dogmatic Investigation of the Sociology of the Church*, it seeks to combine the dialectical theology of Karl Barth with the religious sociology of Ernst Troeltsch. Already in this work the discerning critic can discover indications of Bonhoeffer's later theological positions, such as his rejection of religious individualism, his incarnational vision of the

Church, and his all-embracing Christology. Most significantly, perhaps, this early thesis keeps in dynamic tension the divine and human aspects of the Church, the theological and the sociological dimensions of ecclesiology, without sacrificing either to the other.

This thesis, published at Bonhoeffer's own expense in 1930, attracted little attention at the time, but in 1955 Karl Barth was to write of it:

If there is any justification for Reinhold Seeberg, it may well be this: out of his school came this man and this dissertation, which wins our deepest respect thanks to the width and depth of its vision. . . . I admit that I have trouble even in keeping up to the standard which Bonhoeffer set in those days, and in not saying less, or speaking more weakly, from my own perspective and in my own language than this young man did at that time.[3]

After a year as curate to the German colony in Barcelona, Bonhoeffer returned to Berlin and wrote in 1929–30 a graduate thesis on *Act and Being*. From his Lutheran standpoint, Bonhoeffer is critical of the one-sidedly actualistic approach to revelation and grace characteristic of Karl Barth. The dialectical theologians, in his view, atomize too much God's presence with men. Bonhoeffer maintains that in the Church, as the Body of Christ, God is with His people not simply by occasional action but by a stable communion of being.

In 1930–31 Bonhoeffer spent a year in New York at Union Theological Seminary. Although he admired Reinhold Niebuhr, he formed a rather low opinion of the general state of theology in the United States. He spent his Sundays in Harlem and there became devoted to Negro spir-

[3] *Kirchliche Dogmatik* 4/2 (Zollikon-Zurich, 1955) 725.

ituals. In a memorandum on his American experience, significantly entitled "Protestantism without Reformation," he observed, almost parenthetically: "The solution to the negro problem is one of the decisive future tasks of the white churches." [4]

Back in Germany in 1931 he joined the systematics faculty at Berlin, combining his academic activities with various enterprises in the social and cultural field. The general tenor of his teaching during this period can be gathered from the volumes of his lectures on Christology and other subjects which have recently been published in English translation. The victory of the Nazi party in the 1933 elections profoundly altered the course of his life. Disappointed by the failure of German Lutheranism to resist the Nazi church-legislation, he resigned his post in 1934 and went to London, where he became involved in the ecumenical Life and Work movement.

The next year he returned to Germany to set up at Finkenwalde a kind of religious community for seminarians and newly-ordained ministers. The weakness of his fellow churchmen in the face of persecution had convinced Bonhoeffer that the purely intellectual kind of university training offered to seminarians was inadequate. About this time he wrote to a friend:

The whole ministerial education today belongs to the Church—monastic-like schools in which pure doctrine, the Sermon on the Mount, and the liturgy are taken seriously. In the university all

[4] *No Rusty Swords* (New York: Harper & Row, 1965) pp. 113 f.

three are not taken seriously, and it is impossible to do so under present circumstances.[5]

The isolation of the community at Finkenwalde was ordered not so much toward personal perfection as toward future apostolic work. "Not monastic seclusion," he wrote, "but concentration for life outside, this is the goal." These words aptly sum up the ideals of the new foundation (it was to be suppressed by the Nazis in 1937) and those of Bonhoeffer himself at this particular stage of his career.

Theologically, the period from 1933 to 1939 has been well characterized by Bethge as the "return to the narrow path." It was a period of deep concentration in which he pondered the full implications of the following of Christ. From the beginning of this period comes his masterly work *The Cost of Discipleship,* in which he criticizes the Lutheran doctrine of justification by faith alone, as it has usually been interpreted, and insists that the Christian is obliged to take up his cross in the footsteps of Christ. "We Lutherans," he charges, "have gathered like eagles round the carcase of cheap grace, and there we have drunk of the poison which has killed the life of following Christ." [6] This book was to be praised by Karl Barth in 1955 as the best yet written on how to shape our lives by the example of Jesus Christ as sketched in the Gospels:

The matter is handled with such depth and precision that I am almost tempted to reproduce them [the opening sections] in an extended quotation. For I cannot hope to say anything better on

[5] Cf. Eberhard Bethge, "The Challenge of Dietrich Bonhoeffer's Life and Theology," *Chicago Theological Seminary Register* 51/2 (Feb., 1961) 23.

[6] New York: Macmillan Paperback, 1963, p. 57.

the subject than what is here said by a man who, having written on discipleship, was ready to achieve it in his own life, and did in his way achieve it even to the point of death.[7]

The other book which belongs to this period is entitled *Life Together*. It is a volume of reflections on community life and prayer for the benefit of the brotherhood at Finkenwalde, some of whose members did not take kindly to the regime of meditation, confession, and liturgical life which Bonhoeffer prescribed. In 1940, when Bonhoeffer became a guest at the Benedictine Abbey at Ettal, he was surprised to find that his *Cost of Discipleship* and *Life Together* were being used as table reading for the monks.

With 1940 we enter the last decisive period of struggle in Bonhoeffer's life. It is prefaced by a brief excursion to America in 1939. Staying once again at Union Theological Seminary, he soon reached the decision expressed in a letter to Reinhold Niebuhr:

I have come to the conclusion that I have made a mistake in coming to America. I must live through this difficult period of our national history with the Christian people of Germany. I will have no right to participate in the reconstruction of Christian life after the war if I do not share the trials of this time with my people.[8]

From 1940 to 1943 he worked secretly with an underground organization which was seeking, with the assistance of highly-placed intelligence officers, to overthrow Hitler. Bonhoeffer was one of the minority of the Christian resistance who actively urged the assassination of Hitler. A

[7] *Kirchliche Dogmatik* 4/2, 604.
[8] Text in D. Bonhoeffer, *Gesammelte Schriften* 1 (Munich: Kaiser, 1958) 320.

number of Bonhoeffer's relatives, including his older brother Claus, were involved in this plot. He was arrested by the Gestapo in April, 1943, and executed two years later, in 1945. A fellow prisoner, the English intelligence officer Payne Best, tells the story of the last Sunday, April 8th:

Pastor Bonhoeffer held a little service and spoke to us in a manner which reached the hearts of all, finding just the right words to express the spirit of our imprisonment and the thoughts and resolutions which it had brought. He had hardly finished his last prayer when the door opened and two evil-looking men in civilian clothes came in and said: "Prisoner Bonhoeffer, get ready to come with us." Those words "Come with us"—for all prisoners they had come to mean one thing only—the scaffold. We bade him good-by —he drew me aside—"This is the end," he said. "For me the beginning of life," and then he gave me a message to give, if I could, to the Bishop of Chichester, a friend to all evangelical pastors in Germany.[9]

Several days later he was hanged.

This last period, from 1940 to 1945, during which he was forbidden to publish, and in which he wrote no complete books, is theologically by far the most significant. During his harried existence as a member of the underground he penned the profound reflections on the Christian's relationship to the world which have since been collected and published as his *Ethics*. And during the lonely days of his imprisonment he expressed in a series of meditative letters his project of setting forth a radically new, nonreligious interpretation of the gospel.

The *Ethics*, as we now have it, is a collection consisting

[9] Quoted in J. D. Godsey, *The Theology of Dietrich Bonhoeffer* (Philadelphia: Westminster, 1960) pp. 202 f.

primarily of four successive approaches to the Christian life written during the years 1940–43. They show a progressively deeper realization of the possibilities of worldly holiness. The key to the book is no doubt its high Christology. Already in the first part, in a chapter on "The Church and the World," we read: "In the face of the Antichrist only one thing has force and permanence, and that is Christ Himself. . . . He is the centre and strength of the Bible, of the Church, and of theology, but also of humanity, of reason, of justice, and of culture." [10] And again: "The more exclusively we acknowledge and confess Christ as our Lord, the more fully the wide range of His dominion will be disclosed to us" (p. 58).

In the second part of this book Bonhoeffer outlines a striking theory of "ethics as formation"—that is, as living according to the concrete form which Christ wills to assume among us here and now. "Ethics as formation," he maintains, "is possible only upon the foundation of the form of Jesus Christ which is present in His Church. The Church is the place where Jesus Christ's taking form is proclaimed and accomplished" (p. 88). The Church, according to Bonhoeffer, must accept a heavy share of responsibility for the drift of modern civilization toward the abyss of nothingness, and is confronted by an unparalleled task in being called upon to prove the lordship of Christ to a world that has become hostile to Him (p. 109).

In the third part, written about the end of 1940, Bonhoeffer develops some of the ideas most characteristic of his last phase, and most essential for understanding the *Prison Letters*. One of these ideas is that of the "penultimate," or

[10] *Ethics* (New York: Macmillan Paperback, 1963) p. 56.

the things before the last things. Through the Incarnation of God, he argues, the natural life has become the penultimate, which is directed toward the grace of justification, which is the ultimate. The Christian cannot choose between the ultimate and the penultimate; they reinforce each other. To give bread to a hungry man for a right motive is to act in the sphere of the penultimate; and it prepares the way for the ultimate, for the coming of Christ.

In the last part of the *Ethics* Bonhoeffer develops a type of cosmic Christology which cannot help reminding the Catholic reader of Teilhard de Chardin and of the magnificent text from *Gaudium et spes* (n. 45, quoted above, p. 76) on Christ as the Alpha and Omega of the universe. Bonhoeffer writes (p. 213):

The will of God, which became manifest and was fulfilled in Jesus Christ, embraces the whole of reality. One can gain access to this whole, without being torn asunder by its manifold variety, only in faith in Jesus Christ, "in whom dwelleth all the fulness of the Godhead bodily" (Col 2:9 and 1:19), "by whom all things are reconciled, whether they be things in earth or things in heaven" (Col 1:20), and whose body, the Church, is "the fulness of Him that filleth all in all" (Eph 1:23).

On the basis of this all-embracing Christology Bonhoeffer rejects what he calls any "static opposition" between the spiritual and the secular; he refuses to think in terms of "two spheres." According to the New Testament doctrine of the Church, he maintains, "all men are taken up, enclosed, and borne within the body of Christ." And even if we define the Church more narrowly as the congregation of the faithful, its function is not to separate itself from the world but to summon the world into the fellowship of the Body of Christ, to which in truth it already belongs. The Church is divided from the world "solely by the fact that she affirms in faith the reality of God's acceptance of man, a reality which is the property of the whole world" (p. 206).[11]

Reflecting on the solidarity between Christ, the Church, and mankind, Bonhoeffer then develops the category of "deputyship" as a fundamental theological principle. Jesus, our life, existed in deputyship for us as the Incarnate Son of God, and therefore all human life becomes in Him essentially a life of deputyship (p. 225). Only the selfless man lives responsibly, and this means that only the selfless man lives. The good life is a life for others, but it does not, Bonhoeffer cautions, regard other men as absolutes. This would be to forget that the real man from whom all humanity derives its true value is the Incarnate God, Jesus Christ. "In Jesus Christ, the real man, the whole of reality is taken up and comprised together; in Him it has its origin, its essence, and its goal" (p. 229).

These brief observations concerning the *Ethics* must suffice for present purposes. They are necessary as a background for what has to be said about Bonhoeffer's last and most challenging work, the famous *Letters and Papers from Prison*.[12] In the last half of this volume he frequently speaks of a new project which is ceaselessly at work in his mind—a nonreligious interpretation of Christianity. The

[11] Bonhoeffer's cosmic view of the Church in the light of the cosmic Christ may profitably be compared with that of Heinrich Schlier cited in chapter 1 of this book; cf. above, p. 13.

[12] This work will be cited according to the pagination in the Macmillan Paperback edition, 1962.

interpretation of the gospel which has been traditional since the earliest centuries is religious; it rests upon the premise that man is a religious animal, one who naturally gravitates toward some reality above and beyond this world. But we are now learning, according to Bonhoeffer, that this religious premise is not an a priori form of the human spirit as such; rather it was a time-conditioned phenomenon. In the past few centuries the sphere of religion has been constantly contracting, and now we are entering an age in which men "simply cannot be religious any more" (p. 162). This means that "the linchpin has been removed from the whole structure of our Christianity to date." We are suddenly faced by the problem, how to speak of God to completely secular men. How can Christ become Lord even of those with no religion? (p. 163)

Bultmann had already taken some dramatic steps toward secularization in his "demythologizing" the New Testament, but in Bonhoeffer's opinion he had gone only halfway, because he failed to see that it was not only the myths but the entire message of the New Testament that had to be reinterpreted for modern man. Even Bultmann's program rested, in the last analysis, on the religious premise of Liberal Protestantism.

In speaking of the immense project he has in mind, Bonhoeffer can do little more than stammer. All the traditional language of Christian proclamation seems to him to have become questionable (p. 187):

Atonement and redemption, regeneration, the Holy Ghost, the love of our enemies, the cross and resurrection, life in Christ and Christian discipleship—all these things have become so problematic and so remote that we hardly dare any more to speak of them. In the traditional rite [of baptism] . . . we are groping after something new and revolutionary without being able to understand it or utter it yet.

Thus Christianity must remain for a time to a large extent a hidden affair, in which we express our faith more in deeds than in articulate speech.

Bonhoeffer's project, as I understand it, rests upon a double thesis, negative and positive. The negative thesis is that Christianity is not, and should not be regarded as, a religion. The positive thesis is that it can and should be worldly. Each of these theses must be examined.

For his views about religion Bonhoeffer relies heavily on the early Barth, who had held that Christianity, far from being one of the world's religions, issues a death warrant against all religion. Religion for Barth meant a product of human aspiration, the highest fulfilment of human possibilities. But Christianity is not a human achievement at all. Rather, he held, it is the word of God which teaches man the sinfulness and pride of all his strivings to rise to the divine by his own efforts.

At various points in the *Prison Letters* Bonhoeffer indicates how he personally understands "religion." The religious man, he says, is one who looks for the divine not in the midst of this world but in a sphere beyond. Salvation is conceived by the religious man as deliverance from this world. God is viewed as someone who must be there in order to provide solutions to human problems, protection for human weakness, refuge from human dangers. Religion, therefore, becomes a boundary phenomenon; it enters the scene where human resources fail. The domain of the religious is a special department of experience, alongside of secular activities. Religion unfolds in the sphere of inwardness and subjectivity. It is characterized by individualism and introspectiveness.

Once this conception of religion is understood, it is easy to see why Bonhoeffer maintains that modern man, at his best, is nonreligious. With the progressive development of human knowledge and techniques, a continually smaller province remains for religion. The trend of modern history has been to subtract more and more things from religious control. Science no longer relies on God as a working hypothesis, as it did in Newton's time. The same may be said, Bonhoeffer argues, of politics, ethics, and philosophy. It is no longer possible to look upon God as a secret power to be invoked when the known forces fail.

In this connection Bonhoeffer makes his famous statement that modern man has come of age. By the disposition of God Himself, he argues, man is now responsible for himself and for the world in which he lives. "God is teaching us that we must live as men who can get along very well without him" (p. 219). This is the tremendous fact of our times which calls for a total reinterpretation of the gospel.

The temptation of official Christianity, says Bonhoeffer, is to resist the adulthood of the world and to try to force man back into a state of childishness. "Efforts are made to prove to a world thus come of age that it cannot live without the tutelage of God" (p. 195). Christian apologetics takes the line that, even if all secular problems can be taken care of by man himself, there still remain ultimate questions, such as death, guilt, and sin, for which religious ministries are required. Bonhoeffer, however, dismisses this apologetical maneuver to capitalize on human weakness as pointless, ignoble, and un-Christian (pp. 196 f.):

Pointless, because it looks to me like an attempt to put a grown-up back into adolescence, i.e., to make him dependent on things on which he is not in fact dependent any more. . . . Ignoble, because this amounts to an effort to exploit the weakness of man for purposes alien to him and not freely subscribed to by him. Un-Christian, because for Christ Himself is being substituted one particular stage in the religiousness of man. . . .

But what alternative does Bonhoeffer propose? As he scrawls his fragmentary letters in his dreary prison cell, he is quite conscious of being able to make only the barest beginning of the "worldly" reinterpretation of the biblical concepts which he regards as necessary. The Church today, he finds, is in a situation somewhat like that of Judeo-Christianity in the first century, when it was first perceived that obedience to God did not necessarily involve the observance of the Mosaic Law.

As an illustration of what he means by worldly reinterpretation, Bonhoeffer discusses the concept of salvation. A religious interpretation would look upon Christianity as one of the religions which seek salvation through a release from this world, so that the emphasis falls on the far side of the boundary drawn by death (p. 205). But is this really the distinctive feature of Christianity as proclaimed by the Gospels and St. Paul? "I am sure that it is not," replies Bonhoeffer; "the difference between the Christian hope of resurrection and a mythological hope is that the Christian hope sends a man back to his life on earth in a wholly new way" (*ibid.*). Frequently in his letters he points out that the Old Testament makes much of health, vigor, and earthly fortune as being included in the effects of God's blessing. And in the New Testament, Jesus claims the whole of human life for Himself. He healed the sick and restored strength to the weak. Sickness and death in the New Testament are regarded as effects of sin, even of individual sin (1 Cor 11:30). Nothing that the gospel has to say about the Cross negates the fact that life, health, and strength are authentic blessings willed by God (cf. pp. 210, 231, etc.).

Bonhoeffer, therefore, refuses to seek God or the kingdom of God through any kind of withdrawal from the world. God's transcendence, he insists, does not imply remoteness from things, but on the contrary makes Him immediately present everywhere. He is "the beyond in the midst." In Christ, who is for us the way to God, the divine exists in human form—"not, as in other religions, in animal form—the monstrous, chaotic, remote and terrifying—nor yet in abstract form—the absolute, metaphysical, infinite, etc."—but Christ is fully and perfectly a man (p. 238). He comes not as an ascetic seeking perfection in the desert, but as one who lives responsibly, that is to say, for others. To be a Christian, therefore, does not mean to be religious in a particular way, but to live responsibly as a man (p. 223). Elsewhere Bonhoeffer says even more pointedly: "This is what I mean by worldliness—taking life in one's stride, with all its duties and problems, its successes and failures, its experiences and helplessness. It is in such a life that we throw ourselves utterly into the arms of God and participate in his sufferings in the world and watch with Christ in Gethsemane" (p. 226). This sentence magnificently combines two distinctive traits of Bonhoeffer's piety: his straightforward worldliness and his almost mystical devotion to Christ crucified.

It is not difficult to see why Bonhoeffer's program of a religionless Christianity has had an enormous resonance in our day. For one thing, the disarming honesty with which he exposes his own doubts, gropings, and convictions is immediately appealing to a generation which is justifiably resentful of the types of ecclesiastical humbug that have come to surround conventional discussions about religion. Bonhoeffer cuts through all this (pp. 238 ff.):

What do we really believe? I mean, believe in such a way as to stake our whole lives upon it? . . . Antiquated controversies, especially those between the different confessions . . . may at any time be revived with passion, but they no longer carry real conviction. . . . Christianity does not stand or fall by these issues. Barth and the Confessing Church have encouraged us to entrench ourselves behind the "faith of the Church," and evade the honest question, what is our real and personal belief? Hence lack of fresh air, even in the Confessing Church.

The term "lack of fresh air" reminds us of something a recent pope is reported to have said about opening the windows of the Church! And it also recalls several statements of Paul VI about an honest dialogue between the Church and the modern world. In an age when Catholics are writing books about such topics as "honesty in the Church," we cannot evade questions such as Bonhoeffer here asks. This does not, of course, mean (nor would Bonhoeffer wish to imply) that the faith of the individual is a purely personal achievement, arrived at without entering into the "faith of the Church" or the historic decisions by which the Church has articulated its faith.

Bonhoeffer's insistence that the Church must once more take on the form of servant likewise foreshadows the most vigorous currents in contemporary Catholicism. While his statements are certainly more vehement than those of Vatican II as set forth in the preceding chapter, they reflect something of the same concern. He writes, for instance (p. 239):

> The Church is her true self only when she exists for humanity. As a fresh start she should give away all her endowments to the poor and needy. The clergy should live solely on the free-will offerings of their congregations, or possibly engage in some secular calling. She must take her part in the social life of the world, not lording it over men, but helping and serving them. She must tell men, whatever their calling, what it means to live in Christ, to exist for others.

In our day many Christians, including Catholics, feel somewhat embarrassed about the negative history of the relations between the Church and the secular order over the past five centuries. Bonhoeffer was right in protesting that the Church had tended to build a separate world for itself and had then carried on a disedifying power-struggle with the "secular" world. Too often official Christianity has been indifferent toward worldly progress, belittled its importance, or striven to exploit it for apologetic purposes. The whole thrust of contemporary Christianity is to seek a deeper engagement with the world. The Church, without forgetting its distinctive mission, is seeking to achieve a more positive relationship with the course of secular history. Bonhoeffer, who so powerfully called for this involvement, deserves the close study he is now receiving.

Another point which Bonhoeffer perceived with prophetic clarity was the increasing difficulty of communicating the Christian message to contemporary man. Christian orthodoxy, as represented by figures such as Barth, was in Bonhoeffer's opinion guilty of "revelational positivism." Ensconcing themselves behind the traditional vocabulary of biblical and dogmatic theology, churchmen said to the world, in effect: this is the message; take it or leave it. Given these alternatives, modern secular man can only leave the message as something incomprehensible and un-enlightening. Bonhoeffer would have been encouraged to hear Pope John XXIII, in 1962, call for a restatement of the Christian message in "the literary forms of modern thought." Such a restatement evidently demands a careful reinterpretation of the biblical terms and concepts, and Bonhoeffer's groping efforts in this direction should pro-vide at least a helpful stimulus.

We must also praise Bonhoeffer for having understood that we are entering a time when it is increasingly difficult for the Christian to speak about the realities of his faith. "That is our own fault,' wrote Bonhoeffer (pp. 187 f.):

During these years the Church has fought for self-preservation as though it were an end in itself, and has thereby lost its chance to speak a word of reconciliation to mankind and to the world at large. So our traditional language must perforce become powerless and remain silent, and our Christianity today will be confined to praying for and doing right by our fellow men. . . . It is not for us to prophesy the day, but the day will come when men will be called again to utter the word of God with such power as will change and renew the world.

This explanation of the present weakness of Christian wit-ness contains much truth. The collective selfishness of the Church, both past and present, is surely one reason why it finds itself unable to utter a prophetic word that will bring multitudes to repentance and new life. We must patiently accept a certain inarticulateness and ineffectivness, and seek to remove its causes by the kind of self-effacing service which Bonhoeffer in his last writings advocated. "It is not abstract argument," he wisely commented, "but concrete example which gives her word emphasis and power" (p. 240).

But let us now come to the most fundamental question about Bonhoeffer. Was he correct in thinking that we are entering an age in which religion would be obsolete? And if so, was he right in interpreting this theologically as something positively ordained by God? Can there be and should there be a religionless Christianity?

In great part this depends upon one's concept of religion. Bonhoeffer, as we have noted, defines the term in a narrow and pejorative sense derived from Feuerbach and Barth. Religion is for him a matter of privacy and inwardness, a turning to God to supplement the inadequacies of the world. If Christianity is defined in terms of religion in this sense, it is necessarily hostile to the progress of the secular which Bonhoeffer quite rightly applauded. But this definition fails to do justice to the traditional understanding of religion. By rights the term embraces the whole of man's activity in consciously relating himself to God, whether in private or in public, whether in adoration or in obedient service. "Religion pure and undefiled before God is this: to give aid to orphans and widows in their tribulation, and to keep oneself unspotted from this world" (James 1:27). If religion is taken as including "costly discipleship," surely Bonhoeffer would be the last to dismiss it as a passing phenomenon, antithetical to genuine Christianity.

Formal prayer and worship will always have a place in Christianity, as they did in the life of Bonhoeffer. In the very letters in which he outlines his project of "taking stock of Christianity" he asks his friends to pray for him and assures them of the support of his own prayers. He continues to read and meditate on the Bible, and when possible holds services of worship for his fellow prisoners. If he criticizes religion, then, it is not with any idea of eliminating these exercises of devotion. No doubt he denies them a place of the very first importance in Christianity, but this agrees well with the Gospel precept that it is better to leave one's gift unoffered at the altar than to offer it without being reconciled with one's brother (Mt 5:23 f.).

When men speak of the decline of religion, they are often thinking of the trend toward desacralization which we have outlined in our last chapter. In the course of this process many of the traditional forms of piety are being legitimately questioned and revised, and certain sacral forms may be expected to perish. But this is hardly a symptom of the demise of religion in the sense in which we have defined it. A glance at the contemporary intellectual scene seems to suggest that interest in the questions of God and ultimate values remains vigorous, at least among those who are not thoughtless and superficial. Bonhoeffer himself was ceaselessly concerned with these matters.

Still he does make the very puzzling statement that today God is allowing Himself to be edged out of the world (p. 219). What can this possibly mean coming from the pen of one who insists that God's place is not at the borders of reality but in the midst? How does God get displaced from the midst? And who is edging Him out of the world? The problem is compounded when Bonhoeffer compares this ejection of God with the crucifixion of Christ. Does he mean to align himself with Christ's crucifiers? Is he applauding the death of God? At one point he writes almost atheistically that modern man can get along without the God-hypothesis. "God is teaching us that we must live as men who can get along without him" (p. 219). The correct interpretation of these baffling statements is by no means easy.

From everything else that Bonhoeffer says, even in the letters in which these statements occur, it is clear that he is not pleading for theoretical or practical atheism. He was concerned to establish the autonomy of the world against ecclesiastical encroachments, but before God, he maintained, "there is no autonomy" (*Ethics*, p. 362). Reflecting on the antinomy of autonomy and heteronomy, he suggested that it could be resolved into a higher unity which he called "Christonomy" (p. 299). Many difficult passages in the *Prison Letters* can be illuminated if we regard them as applications of his principle that the law of God is that which comes to us in Jesus Christ. Just as Christ does not wield earthly power, so God, in Bonhoeffer's view, does not allow Himself to be used as a source of worldly might. Just as Christ refuses to answer political and scientific questions, so God cannot be appealed to for such solutions. In this sense God forces us to get along without Him.

Paradoxically, however, it is only the Christian believer who can get along in the world without God. Bonhoeffer was profoundly convinced that we need the God who makes Himself known in Christ in order to see with clear eyes the ungodliness and Godforsakenness of the world. In Christ we can love the world without confusing it with God. The Incarnation enables us to share in God's love for the world, whereas the sight of Christ crucified delivers us from any temptation to divinize it. "Genuine worldliness is possible solely and exclusively on the basis of the proclamation of the cross of Jesus Christ" (*Ethics*, p. 298).

Bonhoeffer was strongly critical of an apologetics which would seek to strengthen the Church by withdrawing men from a responsible participation in the world. But in his later writings he seems to lay the groundwork for another type of apologetics based on the liberating power of faith. Observing the reactions of his fellow prisoners during the Allied air raids, he remarks on the power of Christian belief to give man a sense of the wholeness of life. The unbeliever inevitably lives a fragmented and unstable existence, whereas Christianity plunges us simultaneously into the many dimensions of life. The believing Christian can make room in his heart for God and for the whole world. His sense of life is multidimensional and polyphonous. The divine and the worldly are present to him without separation and without confusion, as the divinity and humanity are combined in the one person of Jesus Christ. The distinction of natures and the unity of person, as affirmed in the Chalcedonian dogma, provided Bonhoeffer with a clue to the dialectical relationship between the worldly features of life and their transcendent ground.

The metaphor of "polyphony" clarifies some of Bonhoeffer's assertions concerning the total absence of God in the realm of earthly objects and His sustaining presence in the realm of selfless love. In music, he remarks, there must be a good, clear *cantus firmus* to give firm support to the counterpoint and to keep it from getting out of tune. And only a polyphony of this sort can give life a wholeness. God, who requires us to love Him eternally with our whole hearts, and yet so as not to compromise or diminish our earthly affections, must provide the *cantus firmus* of our lives. Earthly affection becomes one of the contrapuntal themes—a theme sustained by the rich ground bass of the love of God.

It would be misleading to press Bonhoeffer's statement, that we must live in the world as though there were no God, as if it were an unparadoxical summation of his whole theology. The phrase "etsi deus non daretur" comes into his writing as a quotation from the seventeenth-century natural-law theologian Hugo Grotius, and harmonizes very imperfectly with Bonhoeffer's radical Christocentrism. If Bonhoeffer maintained that "the God who is with us is the God who forsakes us" (*Prison Papers*, p. 219), he was equally confident of the converse—that the God who forsakes us is always present with us. This is strikingly expressed in one of his last letters (p. 243):

The key to everything is the [Pauline expression] "in him." All that we rightly expect from God and pray for is to be found in Jesus Christ. . . . We must always live close to the presence of God, for that is newness of life; and then nothing is impossible and all things are possible in God; no earthly power can touch us without his will, and danger can only drive us closer to him. We can claim nothing for ourselves, and yet we may pray for everything. Our joy is hidden in suffering, our life in death. But all through we are sustained in a wondrous fellowship.

Bonhoeffer's program for a nonreligious Christianity, then, is by no means a denial of the transcendent or the divine. He does not look upon God as a competing reality alongside or above earthly powers, for this would make Him an alien power and subject the world to heteronomy. But it would be equally fallacious in his eyes to repudiate God in order to affirm the world. This would make an absolute out of the relative, an ultimate out of the penultimate, and would eventuate in an idolatrous deification of the world. In Christ Bonhoeffer finds the God who forsakes the world, and thereby gains the strength to live and die in Christlike dereliction. This union with the suffering Christ enabled Bonhoeffer to exclaim, as he left for the scaffold: "This is the end. . . . For me, the beginning of life."

Bonhoeffer's mysticism of the Cross offers one of the most powerful remedies that can be prescribed for contemporary man, oppressed by the emptiness of the world and the seeming absence of God. The anguished man of our day, in revolt against the fatuous, benevolent deity of nineteenth-century optimism, still feels the attractive power of Christ's sacrificial love and responds readily to His call to "costly discipleship." Bonhoeffer sketched with incomparable power the lineaments of Christ as "the man for others." With ruthless honesty and sober realism he recalled the Church from its pompous dreams of grandeur to its task of humble witness and devoted service. He longed for an open, penitent, self-effacing Church, and many sincere Christians today share that longing.

The limitations in Bonhoeffer's theology come more from his omissions than from his assertions. In tendency he is, like Barth, decidedly mono-Christic; he speaks continually of Christ, but only rarely of the Father and of the Holy Spirit. While he unquestioningly accepts the full divinity of Christ, he is reticent about it, and prefers to dwell on the fulness of Christ's humanity. In his theology of redemption he puts so much weight on the restoration of man's human existence that he neglects the other theme so dear to the Greek Fathers—that of man's elevation to the divine.

Most notable in his later works is spiritual concentration on the Cross, which he quite rightly interpreted as a sign that God loves the world in spite of its ungodliness, and that we should do likewise. But a theology of the Cross, however profound, is incomplete unless supplemented by a theology of glory. The heart of the Christian message since Pentecost is precisely that the Cross, in spite of all appearances, is not the last word. The Lamb who has been slain now reigns in glory; He whom the world rejected has come to dwell in it again. Present through His Holy Spirit, He is daily at work renewing the world. Christ does not merely accept our sinful humanity. By His grace He transforms us from within and gives us a share in His own divine Sonship.

These lacunae in Bonhoeffer's theology are partly due to the particular tradition in which he worked, and perhaps even more to the troubled times and the brevity of his career. They in no way diminish the greatness of the bold germinal insights on which we have dwelt in this chapter. He was far in advance of his contemporaries. In spite of the enormous achievements of Vatican Council II, it will probably take generations before we can say that we have fully learned what Bonhoeffer has to teach us. His pithy, unadorned prose, which compresses so much power into a few words, is the literary counterpart of his unaffected style of life and the simplicity with which he chose to follow the rough path which God had marked out for him.

★ Epilogue ★

Our reflections in these pages took their departure from the observation that Catholics ought not to be estranged from the rest of mankind. How has it happened that the faith which most insistently proclaims the unity of all men should itself be a source of division? To some extent this division is inevitable, and may be expected to continue. Christ Himself was a stumbling block for many of those whom He longed to gather into the family of God, and He predicted that His followers would be treated as aliens and enemies. The Christian cannot simply meet the world on its own terms and endorse its own estimate of itself. When he comes proclaiming the good news of Christ, he will normally find the majority of men too preoccupied with temporal affairs to give much heed. Reflecting on the experiences of His own apostolate, Christ composed the parable of the wedding guests who were too busy to come to the great supper to which they had been invited (Lk 14:15–24). Paul, when he announced at Athens the joyful tidings of the Resurrection, received the typical answer, "We will hear you again on this matter" (Acts 17:32). That the same response should be given in our day should not discourage Christians or cause them to dilute the word of God.

But the lack of communication which today exists between the Church and mankind is in part avoidable. Too often the Church has tried to market the gospel wrapped in the language and thought-forms of feudal or baroque Europe. In the past decade the Church has become acutely conscious of the need to update itself and speak in meaningful language to all men of good will. In this way fresh attention has been focused on the horizons of the Church, the border regions at which it comes into contact with the rest of mankind.

In the present study we have explored the types of relationship which arise in these border areas. We have seen that it is theologically unwarranted to look upon men who are not members of the Church as strangers or adversaries, for in Christ all have been united. His grace is operative beyond the visible limits of the Church, and the power of sin is not extinct within the Church. Reality is complex and does not correspond to the simple categories of abstract logic. Everywhere we find that the outside and the inside are strangely intermingled. What appears to be outside the Church is often in some respects within; and what appears to be within the Church may in fact not belong to its true nature. Toward apparent outsiders we must be more respectful and attentive than we once were, and toward ourselves more diffident, more humble, more repentant.

The recent efforts of the Church to relate itself positively toward the other Christians, toward the other religions, and toward the secular aspirations of mankind have on the whole been very well received. The response of Protestant and Orthodox Christians to the ecumenical movement, as promoted by Catholics, has been especially heartening; and the almost universally favorable reaction which has greeted the efforts of the Holy See in the spheres of world peace and social justice has surpassed all expectations. We seem to find ourselves at the beginning of a great new dialogue which offers almost limitless possibilities of revitalization for the Church itself as well as for others who enter into conversation with it.

And yet it must be confessed that this dialogue, so fruitfully initiated, has caught many Catholics unprepared. Trained in abstract and schematic forms of thought, the clergy and much of the laity have become aloof from the world, suspicious of it, disinclined to take it seriously. Fearful of compromise, they have been intransigent even to the point of hostility. Their zeal for purity of faith and morals has often betrayed them into attitudes foreign to the mind and heart of Christ Himself. Those who strive to overcome the narrowness of this heritage sometimes find themselves accused of being "soft on Protestants," of coddling false religions, or of capitulating before the rising tide of secularism.

In these pages we have sought to show that a more positive attitude toward the whole human family is required by fidelity to Christ and the Church. If the Church is the Body of Christ, as we have shown in our first chapter, it must be the unifying center toward which every holy thought and aspiration gravitates as the locus of its fulfilment. And if the Church is made up of sinful, fallible men, it needs advice and criticism from outside its own membership. From the standpoint of this basic view of the relationship between the Church and the human family, we have in the next three chapters studied three crucial areas of intercommunication between the Church and its neighbors. Our conclusions concerning ecumenism, missiology, and Christian secularity have been little more than applications of the general principle that the Church stands in solidarity with all mankind and must be ready to enter into respectful dialogue at every level.

In our final chapter we have dealt with a Protestant theologian whose thinking about the Church was thoroughly ecumenical and in a very true sense "catholic." In his life and writings Bonhoeffer vividly illustrates the heights to which the life of faith, hope, and charity can sometimes rise beyond the visible borders of the Roman Catholic communion. He himself protested against the anachronistic and senseless divisions between Evangelical and Catholic Christianity and strove for a total Christian witness that would be free from every taint of sectarianism.

The popularity of Bonhoeffer among Catholics of the present generation should not surprise us. In pointing out the damage wrought by ecclesiastical egotism, that fountainhead of obscurantism and irrelevance, he speaks of things with which we are all too familiar. A prophetic witness of the open Church, he pleaded with his very life for an organized Christianity which would surrender its pompous claims and dedicate itself generously to binding up the wounds of the human family.

Although Bonhoeffer had little directly to say about missiology, his thought was destined to have great impact on that field. He reflected deeply on the problem of reinterpreting the gospel for contemporary "religionless" man. Successful evangelization, he perceived, requires that Christians should be able to relate themselves positively to the world and its concerns, and should not anchor itself to primitive or superstitious forms of piety. He saw likewise that the Christian life was essentially one of deputyship for others—a point which we have developed in our own exposition of the Church's "catholicity."

Bonhoeffer's most important contribution lay no doubt in his observations on the polarity between the Church and the world in the life of Christians. He has often been presented as the champion of a purely secular Christianity which would seek God exclusively in the world. But if we have analyzed his thought correctly, his God was eminently transcendent. He held that God was by no means continuous with the world; He was not to be sought at its borders or even in its depths. Because God was totally beyond the world and distinct from it, He could be found everywhere. The Christian can therefore relate himself to God without withdrawing from human society and fleeing to the desert.

At least in his later writings Bonhoeffer shies away from the category of the sacred. No doubt the times and circumstances in which he lived called for greater worldliness on the part of men of faith. But our own generation seems to be faced more acutely by the problem how secular men, distracted by innumerable pleasures and concerns, can achieve an intense communion with God and walk unswervingly in the footsteps of Christ. And it is here that the sacred has special application. In our day the sacred is suspect because it is often laden with the religiosity of a bygone age. Not infrequently the secular institutions of the past are presented as if they had some sacred aura about them. In such cases the allegedly sacred cannot effectively nourish the inner life of modern man and send him back to the world with greater vision and strength.

In order that the Church may give more effective divine guidance and bring men more vitally into communion with God, great attention must be paid to the inner renewal of the Church as a confessing and worshiping community. The recent Council perceived this, and devoted much of its most important work to the revitalization of doctrine, liturgy, and the structures of the religious life. Although the preceding pages have concentrated primarily on the relationship of the Church to the rest of the human family, it should be kept in mind that the Church's own inner transformation is of decisive importance if the face of the earth is to be renewed.

★ Index of Authors ★

A

Augustine, St. 19, 20

B

Balthasar, H. U. von 81
Barth, K. viii, 88, 89, 91, 102, 105, 110
Baum, G. 33
Bellarmine, R. 4–6, 9
Bergson, H. 2, 3
Best, P. 93
Bethge, E. 91
Bonhoeffer, D. viii, ix, 47, 71, 87–111, 115, 116
Bosc, J. 39
Botte, B. 57
Bultmann, R. ix, 97

C

Calvin, J. 22
Chenu, M.-D. 81
Congar, Y. 31
Cox, H. 66, 67, 87

F

Feeney, L. 10
Feuerbach, L. 105

G

Grotius, H. 109

H

Hamilton, W. 87
Hermas 16
Hillman, E. 53, 54
Hoekendijk, J. C. 45

I

Irenaeus, St. 27, 28, 50

J

John XXIII 18, 21, 29, 40, 104

L

Luther, M. 22, 69, 70

M

Malmberg, F. 5
Mascall, E. L. 66
Mehta, V. 87
Molinari, P. 18

N

Newton, I. 99
Niebuhr, R. 89, 92
Novak, M. 3

P

Paul VI 3, 6, 102
Pius IX 23, 24
Pius XI 25
Pius XII 8, 10, 24, 60

R

Rahner, K. 47, 75, 85
Robinson, J. A. T. 87

S

Schillebeeckx, E. 13, 15
Schlier, H. 13, 96
Seeberg, R. 88, 89
Söderblom, N. 38
Stransky, T. 32, 36
Suenens, L. J. 21

T

Teilhard de Chardin, P. 75, 95
Tillich, P. 47
Troeltsch, E. 88

V

van Buren, P. 66, 87
Villain, M. 39
Vischer, L. 40